THE CASTIN(

CREATING A MAGICKAL LIFE
THROUGH THE WORDS
OF TRUE WILL

BY

CHRISTOPHER PENCZAK

Book One of the Magickal Craft Series

**COPPER
CAULDRON**
PUBLISHING

Credits

Editing: Stevie Grant

Proofreading: Karen Ainsworth, Michael Cantone, Antonella Ercolani, Claire Manning, Kathy Pezok, Leeon Pezok, Alura Rose, Deborah Stelhorn, and Raye Snover

Cover Design: Rory McCracken and Terra Nova Creative

Layout & Publishing: Steve Kenson

For more information visit:
www.christopherpenczak.com
www.coppercauldronpublishing.com

ISBN 978-1-940755-07-6, First Printing

Printed in the U.S.A.

Acknowledgements

Special thanks to Steve and Adam for all their love and support in all things.

Thank you to my first mentors in the Craft, showing me how to write and speak my first spell. It was life-changing!

Other Books by Christopher Penczak

City Magick (Samuel Weiser, 2001, 2nd Edition 2012)

Spirit Allies (Samuel Weiser, 2002)

The Inner Temple of Witchcraft (Llewellyn Publications, 2002)

The Inner Temple of Witchcraft CD Companion (Llewellyn Publications, 2002)

Gay Witchcraft (Samuel Weiser, 2003)

The Outer Temple of Witchcraft (Llewellyn Publications, 2004)

The Outer Temple of Witchcraft CD Companion (Llewellyn Publications, 2004)

The Witch's Shield (book with CD) (Llewellyn Publications 2004)

Magick of Reiki (Llewellyn Publications 2004)

Sons of the Goddess (Llewellyn Publications 2005)

The Temple of Shamanic Witchcraft (Llewellyn Publications 2005)

The Temple of Shamanic Witchcraft CD Companion (Llewellyn Publications 2005)

Instant Magick (Llewellyn Publications 2005)

The Mystic Foundation (Llewellyn Publications 2006)

Ascension Magick (Llewellyn Publications 2007)

The Temple of High Witchcraft (Llewellyn Publications 2007)

The Temple of High Witchcraft CD Companion (Llewellyn Publications 2007)

The Living Temple of Witchcraft Volume I (Llewellyn Publications 2008)

The Living Temple of Witchcraft Volume I CD Companion (Llewellyn Publications 2008)

The Living Temple of Witchcraft Volume II (Llewellyn Publications 2009)

The Living Temple of Witchcraft Volume II CD Companion (Llewellyn Publications 2009)

The Three Rays of Witchcraft (Copper Cauldron Publishing 2010)

The Plant Spirit Familiar (Copper Cauldron Publishing 2011)

The Witch's Heart (Llewellyn Publications 2011)

The Gates of Witchcraft (Copper Cauldron Publishing 2012)

Buddha, Christ, and Merlin (Copper Cauldron Publishing 2012)

The Green Lover (editor, Copper Cauldron Publishing 2012)

The Feast of the Morrighan (Copper Cauldron Publishing 2012)

Ancestors of the Craft (editor, Copper Cauldron Publishing 2012)

The Mighty Dead (Copper Cauldron Publishing 2013)

The Waters and Fires of Avalon (editor, Copper Cauldron Publishing 2013)

The Phosphorous Grove (limited edition, Copper Cauldron Publishing 2013)

Foundations of the Temple (Copper Cauldron Publishing 2014)

TABLE OF CONTENTS

INTRODUCTION

I've been living a magickal life for over twenty years, but I started out as a skeptic. When a friend first introduced me to the concept of magick and psychic powers, I honestly thought she was having some sort of nervous collapse due to pressures in her life, being a single mom and business owner. In my effort to help her out of this delusion, I needed to try to understand how she got there and why. The more I discovered—some directly from her and some on my own or through resources she recommended—the more I opened to the possibility that she wasn't suffering from a delusion. Yet I still remained a skeptic. I had left the hard world of dogmatic religion and was not quick to embrace anything without tangible evidence. I approached it as a science, or at the very least, a pseudo-science. I needed some sort of direct experience. Then I got it.

She gave me the opportunity to go to what she called an Esbat, a Full Moon circle. There I was given the opportunity to perform a healing spell for a friend with major health complications due to her pregnancy. She and the baby to be born were both in serious danger if something didn't change very quickly, and the doctors were not hopeful. She gave birth a few weeks after the spell, and to the surprise of everyone, all the potential factors that had to change did. The baby's position shifted. She got the nutrition she needed. The baby's weight increased. Both their vital signs stabilized into normal ranges. And most important, the petition spell, in the style in which I will teach you in this book, stated, "...mother and baby survive, and the labor be as easy as possible." Her labor only lasted two hours. She was up and about soon after, wondering what the big deal was. People were stunned. I knew many people were praying for her, the doctors were great at taking care of her health plan, and she had a very loving family, but the two hours in labor floored me. That's when I decided to give magick some serious consideration, time and effort. I wanted to know more. I wanted to experience more. Dare I say, I hoped it was real and that it could be a life I could lead? Little did I know how much my fate would change that year, and that patterns were set that would serve me for a lifetime.

Since that fateful Moon circle, I've delved into the spiritual side of magick, Witchcraft, shamanism, alchemy and ceremonial magick. I went in the direction I had consciously avoided prior to my magickal experience, but with the skills of a skeptic still at hand. I've become a minister, an author, a teacher and a community leader. I had none of those ambitions at the time. I saw the ritual as divorced from anything specifically spiritual, yet the magick led me to my spirit in a very personal and individual way.

As a teacher, I've had the opportunity to teach a wide variety of workshops and classes, from the simple and practical, to the deeply theological. Yet some of my favorite workshops, which also happen to be the most popular, are not the deep and philosophical classes, but a short series on practical magickal crafting, one night each on spells, candles, potions, charms and symbols. In my opinion, they are life skills everyone should learn, things to empower the self through a harmony and partnership with nature. In the times of crisis of my life, including heartbreak from a disastrous relationship, failure in a final credit check prior to a new mortgage, and a parent's diagnosis of a terminal disease, I don't know what I would have done without magickal skills and spells to help alter the situation and handle it better. The total skeptic might see it all as a placebo, a distraction acting as a coping mechanism, yet I've seen so many miracles of healing and amazing synchronicities that I am utterly convinced in the reality of magick and the principles that govern it. This series of short books, starting with *The Casting of Spells*, is meant to pass on that wisdom with a minimum of the religious traditions of Witchcraft or any other spiritual system. These are simply skills, to be applied in whatever manner you see fit in your own life. I hope they can serve you as well as they have served me.

Chapter One:
What is Magick?

Before we go about casting spells for ourselves or anyone else, we should really understand what they are. There's a saying amongst the teachers of magick: "First you start out studying the magick. Then you go about practicing the magick. Soon you realize you've become the magick." Everything in your life takes on magickal significance and in retrospect, it always has. You just didn't know it. Sadly, many of us jump into the doing magick, make a mistake, and go back to the study, hoping to undo the mistake or start over.

A famous and controversial magician in the twentieth century came up with the most well-known definition of magick in the modern western traditions. His name was Aleister Crowley, and he declared himself the prophet of the New Age. And perhaps he was. With some unusual characteristics that would not be very shocking to us today, such as his free bisexuality, drug use and a heretical sense of humor when it came to Christian orthodoxy, he scandalized his Victorian peers. His name, despite the Ozzy Osbourne song to the contrary, is pronounced in a way that rhymes with "holy" or "unholy," depending on your point of view, and many held either view of him strongly. I'm no Crowley apologist, as he did actually do some quite awful things in his personal life, even if they were not the reasons newspapers declared him the "most wicked man in the world." He was immensely smart, and synthesized a wide range of magickal texts and ideas from his direct studies across the world into his magickal traditions and training. So when he gave us a definition of magick, he knew what he was talking about.

defined magick as "the Science and Art of causing
)ccur in conformity with Will." That's a fancy way of
t you want something to occur and you take action to
:cur. His definition specifically included both acts of
ritual magick that we would recognize as spell casting, charms,
candle magick and spirit summoning, as well as simple, direct
actions. Doing a ritual to get five hundred dollars that you don't
currently have to pay your rent is an act of magick. Going to the
bank and withdrawing five hundred dollars from your own
account is also an act of magick. The first, though, if it succeeds, is
more impressive.

Crowley's definition capitalizes quite a few words – *Magick,
Science, Art, Change,* and *Will*. That means they are significant, and
might not stand for the same word when it's in its lower case form.
The lower case form has a more common and accepted meaning.
The uppercase form is more lofty and spiritual, or at least more
complex. The capital is his clue to you that something is going on.
Or perhaps he just liked to write with a lot of capitals for dramatic
flair.

First, he popularized the use of the archaic form of spelling the
word *magick,* with a k at the end. He did so to distinguish "magick"
from "magic," which he defined as the illusionists' sleight-of-hand
tricks on the stage. He did live in the era of Harry Houdini, who
consequently liked to debunk spiritualist and occultists as frauds,
exposing any who used any form of stage magic. Strangely, many
occultists today are also trained as stage-show magicians, and one
can look at the original occult magicians of the human race, the
first shamans and medicine people, as using sleight-of-hand tricks
in ritual to create certain effects in their work, such as banging
together two pieces of quartz to release a flash of light from their
piezoelectric qualities. Did they believe it was magick or did they

see it as trickery? Was there a distinction between perception and reality at that point in our consciousness? The "k" is also the eleventh letter of the English alphabet, and eleven plays an important role in Crowley's theology and in particular with his disciples that follow in his footsteps. Eleven is the number of *Da'ath* in Hermetic Qabalah. It means knowledge and represents an important and dangerous point in a Hermetic Magician's career and quest for power, knowledge, love and enlightenment.

Science and *Art* are capitalized as, in this new era, he felt magick would take on the role of science, art and religion. The slogan to one of his magickal training groups is "the method of science - the aim of religion." One must look methodically at the data and experiences, and be able to shift paradigms without being dogmatic. *Change* is also capitalized to signify that it is a change in the state of being for the situation or individual.

Most importantly, the word *Will* is capitalized. It is distinguished from "will" with a lower case "w." I once had a teacher, who, when emphasizing the moral teaching of Wicca, the Wiccan Rede, where it states, "Do as ye will and let it harm none," asked me, "How do you spell will?" I repeated several times, *"w-i-l-l."* She then asked me out of frustration if the w was capital or lower case and I said it didn't matter. Of course, she said it did, and began to tell me about True Will.

True Will

Will with a small "w" can also be equated with want or desire, or even need on a personal level. It is originating from the human self, the personality or ego, or from base functions of the body. It is neither good nor bad by itself. We have desires, and magick is a path of fulfilling desires. Hopefully with good magick, this desire leads us to Will with a capital "W," the desire of our Soul, or Higher

Self. Crowley was known to call it either your Holy Guardian Angel, as it is the part of you that is most like an angel, or the Bornless One, the part of you that is never born into the world and thereby never dies. It exists eternally outside of space and time, ever wise and guiding those who will let it and listen. In my own tradition, we call it the Watcher, as that is both a name for a race of Angels associated with Witchcraft, and it is the part of you that observes, that watches or witnesses. Other traditions have other names for it, including Sacred Dove, Alpha, Star Walker or Daemon. It is the part of you that has True Will, and it's your job, as a person in this lifetime, to discover and implement your True Will. Magick done for the highest will is continually pointing you to your True Will, your soul's purpose. It is sacred and holy. Magick done without this intention, this essential element, is hit or miss at best in terms of evolution on a spiritual level.

True Will has correspondences in other traditions as well. In Christianity, it's the real secret behind the phrase, "Thy Will be done." Magicians rile at that phrase, feeling it is sacrificing the will/Will to a distant creator's will, but in essence it means the part of you that is like God that is the will to be done, not the personal or flawed self's will. In Hinduism, we would refer to the results of our actions performed with lower-case will as karma, both good and bad, or more accurately, pleasant and unpleasant, and actions from our True Will as our dharma, our "right action." In Buddhism, dharma is synonymous with the teachings of the Buddha, as they are believed to be the only right actions. They are the behaviors, from a Buddhist perspective, that lead to liberation.

Understanding and exploring the concept of True Will can be quite difficult. If it's not entirely clear for you at this stage, you can certainly still get your hands dirty with spell casting using the techniques of this book. I have to admit I've cast many spells

The Casting of Spells

without having any idea what True Will was at all, in theory, let alone my own True Will. If you do magick from an ethical win-win posture, it will lead you to your True Will, whether you know it or not.

Changes in Consciousness

A contemporary of Crowley's, occultist Dion Fortune, often described as High Priestess to the New Age and he as Prophet, made a slight change in her definition of magick. She said, "Magick is the art of causing changes in consciousness in conformity with Will." She left out the science, used far fewer capitals and most importantly added the words "in consciousness" to the definition. The importance of that part is to realize that to really be effective in magick, you must change something within your own self, your own consciousness, before you can ever change it outside of yourself. The change must come from within.

In occult traditions, there is a teaching called the Principle of Correspondence. Simply stated, it says, "As above, so below. As within, so without." What it really means is that the outer world is a reflection of the inner world, and vice versa. Magick is the art of creating a change within you, and the outer world will ultimately mirror that change. That's the "changes in consciousness" part emphasized by Dion Fortune. She was also into the growing field of psychology and the application of magickal concepts in popular psychology that has become more and more prevalent.

The difficult part about it is that a good magickal teacher will tell you that if you cannot already feel the results of the spell before you begin, you will have a hard time having success. If you want to cast a love spell, you must feel love already in yourself. If you want to cast a good-fortune spell, you must feel lucky or successful when you do. It's a catch-22 situation, because if you felt that way already, you probably are not lacking the very thing that has inspired you to cast the spell. How do you feel it if you are lacking it?

That is where the techniques of spell casting come in. Ritual techniques are a time honored set of traditions, found in their most basic form all around the world because they are common to the human experience, as much as fire, shelter, herbalism and hunting are common to people across the world. Ritual techniques can put you in a space of possibilities and connect you to the very thing you wish to create, thereby creating a change, even momentarily, in consciousness. If you can create your magick from that moment of change, you will be an effective magician.

Arguably, magick is a system or technology that allows us to change our consciousness, and through that consciousness, effect tangible change in our own lives. Some focus almost exclusively on the outer-world manifestations, while others focus on the inner-world personal growth, but one will always affect the other, and eventually you'll notice it, if true change is occurring within your consciousness.

What Are Spells?

So if these are the definitions of magick, what exactly is a spell? A spell can be any specific act of magick. While magick can be a continuous experience, a spell usually has a very definitive intention, with a clear-cut ritual. The ritual has a beginning, middle and end, a set goal and a set of criteria that can measure if the given spell was successful or not. The intention is specific, even if the means by which it might manifest is open to chance. Did it actually do what you intended it to do, with your will and/or Will? If not, why not? Evaluate it, and see if it was faulty spellcraft.

Spells and our idea of "spelling" with letters in sequence are intimately related. Intention that is clearly written or clearly spoken, in common letters or esoteric symbols and tongues, is in reality a spell. When we cast a spell, we are writing it out to the universe. It is like we are writing a letter, spelling out each of the words one by one as we cast the spell. Gods and spirits of magick have traditionally also been associated with language, words, writing and mathematics. The Greeks have Hermes, the messenger and psychopomp who lent his name to the magickal teacher Hermes Trismegistus, philosopher, alchemist and master. Hermes is associated with the Egyptian god Thoth, though his more Egyptian name is Tehuti. Described as an ibis-headed god, he is the scribe of the gods of Egypt. Nabu of Sumeria holds a similar function as scribe. In many traditions, including esoteric Christian ones, creation begins with a sound, the "Word" or Logos. When it is spoken, creation is initiated. We can think of it as an esoteric look at the Big Bang. Even master magicians such as Merlin from Arthurian myth are associated with books of magick, scrolls and laboratories found in a wizard's tower. He is known for speaking his magick words to make things happen.

Sometimes the language we speak in with a spell does not use writing or speaking in a literal sense, but involves actions, symbols, movements or items from the natural world, such as herbs, stones and metals. They are an effective form of magick, but not the focus of our work here.

This book will be focusing primarily on the written and spoken spells, though it's hard to talk about spells in an ethical way without talking about magick, spirituality and evolution. But our focus will be on spells through words, petitions and incantations, written and spoken magick, once the fundamental ideas are explained and understood. Other forms of magick will be explained with other books in this series.

Exercise: What is your True Will?

If someone were to ask you right now, "What is your life's purpose?" what would you say? What's the first thing that comes to mind? Say it out loud. How does it feel? It doesn't have to be right or wrong. It's right and honest in this moment. Write it down somewhere you'll remember it.

If your answer was, "I don't know," you're not alone, and magick can help you explore and refine that over time, but it can be good to know where you currently are to appreciate where you are going.

These ideas are not as esoteric as they sound. We find them in a lot of schools of thought and from practical common sense. Positive thinking and focusing on your goals are two simple ways to apply ideals of magick. Affirmations can be a form of magick. In more esoteric terms, we have self-help things like the Law of Attraction, the Law of Manifestation, or the short-lived but immensely popular book *The Secret*. Making goal lists, using vision boards and even wishing on a star, dandelion puff ball or birthday cake candles are forms of spell casting, if you know what you are doing.

Chapter Two: The Two Sides of Magick

Magick has two distinct sides to it that are necessary to learn if you want to have a successful and meaningful practice. Spells are really only one side of the coin. Since spellcraft is our focus in this book, that's where the majority of our teachings will be centered, but it would be remiss of me not to explain the other side, and to encourage you to investigate it.

If spells are one side of the equation, what is the other? Or perhaps, a better question is, if speaking to the universe your desire and intention in no uncertain terms is one side of the equation, then what is the other? Listening, naturally. If speaking is one half, listening must be the second half of the formula.

Magick can be compared to a conversation you have with the universe, however you view the universe. Many different magicians, all successful at their craft, have very different views on the nature of whatever it is they feel they are communicating with to effectively create magick and cast spells. It's funny that no one belief or dogma seems to bear out effectively as the only truth, but the fact that they have some belief, some system or paradigm, seems to be the common factor.

Many modern magicians realize that systems of magick are just tools, approximations of a truth, but not the truth. Religions have yet to figure that out. You can have many different beliefs about the nature of creation, the universe, divinity and energy, and they can all be right and they can all be wrong. If you are fully immersed in any one for a given moment, it can be effective. I once had a teacher who said, "Witches don't believe. We know." Basically she was saying we don't rely on dogma or religion, but direct experience. If we experience it, it's true for us. We don't need someone to tell us our truth. We seek our own truth.

Your Conversation Partner

For much of this book, I'll be generalizing the force with whom you are conversing in your magickal conversation, or falling back upon my own personal spiritual practice as a modern Witch. The Universe is about as good of a description for this force as any other. You can make it personal or impersonal. Call it by a specific name. Imagine it in a specific nature. But ultimately we don't know. Some common thoughts about this force, this intelligence, if that can even be the right word, include:

Universe – A generalized sense of the life force and awareness of the Universe, seen in either a very personal or impersonal sort of way. Universe is a nice, non-dogmatic or culturally specific way of saying divine intelligence or creative force as we perceive it cosmically. Magick is the art of sending signals to this universal consciousness, and receiving signals from it, like cells within the body sending and receiving signals on the nervous system, and receiving what they need in terms of food, energy, oxygen, and the removal of waste. Many systems of magick and religion see this as the Creator, not separate from the creation. The creation is the body of the Creator, but a divine intelligence permeates it.

Divine Mind – Hermetic magicians often see the cosmos in terms of the Divine Mind. Everything is a thought created within the Divine Mind, a cosmic collective consciousness. Some see this as wise and beneficent and generally with humanity's best interest at heart. Others see it as simply information that responds and reacts, with no sentiment or agenda.

Transcendent Creator – In many traditions, the creative intelligence is separate from the creation. Most traditions of "The

Book", Judaism, Christianity and Islam, see their image of "God" separate from creation, with messengers and forces to interact and intercede on humanity's behalf, from the angels to the saints. Ultimate divinity is impersonal. In Masonic traditions and many other secret societies, the Creative Intelligence is embodied by an architect who creates and sets the universe in motion, but has little to do with it once it has been put into effect.

Specific Entities – Various religions and magickal systems direct their prayers, petitions and spells at specific entities, not always seen as the ultimate creative force or source of life, but as having dominion over a particular facet of life or creation. To effect change in that area of life, you must petition the appropriate spirit, god, angel, demon or djinn, in the correct manner, and your magick will be successful. Such systems are often based, at least fundamentally, on planetary and star correspondences, as the heavenly bodies are seen as intermediating agencies between humanity and the divine intelligence beyond.

Cosmic Forces – In this system, the universe consists of impersonal cosmic forces that follow perceived patterns of behavior. Some would see them as the Yin and Yang of the Taoists of Asia. It is the flow of the "Way." If you can harness the flow, you can create things and receive information. If you can't, life appears to happen to you. In the Teutonic traditions of the West, it is fire and ice coming together as primal forces. When you personalize these cosmic forces, or at least give them more humanized forms, they become the dualism of the Goddess and the God of Witchcraft, or triplicities of divine trinities such as Brahma, Vishnu and Shiva in various forms of Hinduism. Sometimes dualities and triplicities co-exist in one system, with other divisions of divine powers.

Higher Self – For many, the conversation partner is the higher, wiser aspect of the self. Some think of it strictly in psychological terms, ascribing no supernatural powers to this part of yourself. Its power is found in the awareness it has of all the things beyond your conscious mind. Others think of the Higher Self as your soul, the divine part of you. The concept of the soul's divinity is expanded beyond, to the idea that the Higher Self is the "god self" of the individual. Various forms of magick and spirituality are about developing your relationship with this self, at least as a primary practice. The modern interpretation of the Hawaiian Huna system, popularized by Max Freedom Long, which has gone on to influence the Feri tradition of Witchcraft, emphasizes clearing the blocks and building a relationship with this god self, through the intermediary of a secondary, lower self. In ceremonial magick, the Higher Self is known as the Holy Guardian Angel or Bornless One. Much of the work of modern ceremonial magicians is to enter into "knowledge and conversation" with this divine self, and then unite with it.

So magick is truly having a conversation with some higher or deeper power that can help effect change in your consciousness and change in your world. What you ultimately believe it to be seems to be less important than having the actual conversation.

Exercise: Who Is Your Magickal Conversation Partner?

Like the first exercise, ask yourself, "Who is my magickal conversation partner?" When I ask for things in my life, whom do I think is listening? What is listening? How have I defined it? Is that my own idea or the idea of others, other people – family, friends, community, religion, school? If I think about it for myself, how do I see the universe? Is it personal or impersonal? Is it intelligent or simply responsive to stimuli? Is it loving or uncaring?

Understanding your current views, like your True Will, can help you understand how magick evolves and changes you over time.

Effective Magickal Language

If listening and speaking on the part of both parties is the proper way to have a conversation, it is equally important that both parties are also speaking the same language. Magickal systems, symbols, esoteric languages and ritual techniques are ways to make sure that you both declare what language you are speaking in and ensure clear communication. If two people are speaking different languages, there can be listening and speaking, but not effective communication.

Many people who pray regularly but feel they are not heard, are not speaking effectively, and most often, not listening effectively. The religious systems of today's modern, dogmatic and institutional religions do not teach effective methods of prayer and divine communication. Their whole business is really based upon being an intermediary. If you could effectively speak up for yourself, why would you truly need a priesthood? Unless it is a Mystery Tradition with the goal of producing adepts of mystical or magickal attainment, religious institutions are best in social service support, community building and education, but not with effective communication with the divine.

Spells and specific rituals are the way we speak to the universe, a base language. Traditional systems and techniques have a proven track record to which the universal force, whatever it is, responds. In fact, some spells that are repeated the same way over and over again are even more effective than new and personal spells, because the universal force has an obvious understanding of them. It's like a familiar word, order, or request. If someone asks you to do something unusual or unique for them, you have to pay closer attention, and the instructions might be confusing. But if you are driving and you see a red octagon with white letters on a posted sign saying STOP, you know to stop at the white line before going forward. It's a learned but now automatic response. It's like a training you've undergone. Traditional spells are things that others have trained the universe to respond to do.

If spells are speaking, then in what way do we listen to the universe? I would answer, with introspection. And two of the most effective tools for this introspection are meditation and divination.

Meditation

Meditation is quite simply the process of contemplation. Many misunderstandings occur around exactly what is and what isn't involved in meditation. Most lay people have this understanding that meditation means "no thought" at all. They try to do that, without any technique or strategy, they fail and give up on meditation. In truth, meditation is a focused concentration upon something, and in that process, we can find ourselves in a state of no thought, being truly in the moment rather than projecting our hopes, fears and ideas constantly into the future or fixated upon the past. Simple mindfulness is an effective teaching. In that moment of openness and reception, we can have insights, information and perspectives we would not ordinarily have during the course of our fast-paced day-to-day lives.

Many perceive this as our conversation partner's attempt to speak to us through our quiet consciousness. Those who meditate seem more "tuned in" to greater creativity, ideas, problem solving and peace. Often when we have effective communication, we must stop what we are doing to listen. Sadly, so many of us in daily conversation are not really listening, but are thinking about what we shall say next. The universe seems to know when we are doing this, so it stops talking. You have to give it your full attention for it to speak to you.

Meditations can be active or passive, and come in a variety of forms. Some are still and silent. Some use repetitive words. Some use movement as a focus for meditation, from yoga and tai chi to simply walking at an even pace. Repetitive music such as drumming can help induce a meditative state, as well as a variety of herbs and scents. There is no one right way to do it. You have probably done some form of it already, and not called it meditation or been in a place to really listen. The trance techniques used in spell-crafting can be the same exact ones used for meditation, and will be covered in detail in Chapter Four with specific instructions on how to perform them.

As you grow in your magickal practice with spell-crafting, I urge you to cultivate a meditative practice. I think of it as part of a regular health routine, like eating right or exercising. Like going to the gym or performing another vigorous activity, I think you reap the benefits of it through regular practice, ideally at least three times a week for at least ten minutes, if not twenty, in one sitting. Many people have daily meditative practices for an hour or more, and if you have the time, I encourage it.

Some mystical traditions emphasize meditation over ritual and magick, falling on the side of listening more than speaking. While that is fine for those traditions, and I, too, emphasize listening first before speaking too much, a balanced magickal practitioner must learn to do both.

Divination

To divine something usually means to foresee, and implies an inspiration or message from a deity about the future. To the modern practitioner, divination is a practice to gain information in a nonlinear manner about the past, present and future of a situation, or gain insight about the situation, again in a nonlinear manner. To an experienced diviner, time is fluid, with many possibilities to any one situation.

Divination traditions can be basically divided into two types – fixed and unfixed. Fixed systems use a set of symbols that have basically agreed upon meanings, though the interpretation is widely open to debate in any given reading. These systems include the Runes, Tarot, I-Ching, Geomancy, Astrology and Ogham Sticks. Each contains a range of symbols with traditional meanings and often openings for interpretations depend on the amount of symbols chosen, how they are arranged, and the nature of the question. Some fixed systems of divination are more binary, answering questions in a yes or no format. These would include the pendulum, muscle testing and most simply a coin toss.

Unfixed systems use symbols seen far more subjectively. They include reading the images of tea leaves and coffee grounds, clouds, patterns in smoke, stone, or wax in water, or the images conjured in a dark mirror or crystal ball. The symbols are open to interpretation, and sometimes the images of symbol shapes can expand to include full visions as if you are projecting the inner screen of your mind upon the medium. Others don't have such elaborate visions, and when looking into the matter within the chosen medium, simple shapes are suggested by the patterns, and those symbols are interpreted in light of the questions asked. Omens in nature can also be used as a somewhat unfixed system – the weather, flight of birds, animals and plants encountered and the direction of the wind.

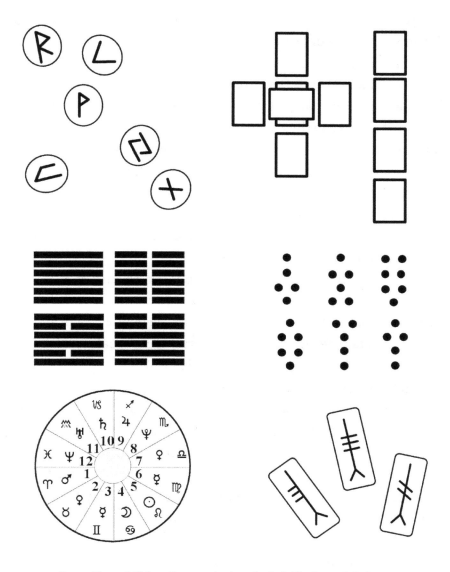

Runes, Tarot, I-Ching, Geomantic, Astrological Glyphs, and Ogham

The benefit of a fixed system is that it is harder, but not impossible, to fool yourself into either seeing what you want to see in the answer to your question, or focusing on your fears and doubts. No matter what the other cards are, it's hard to paint a completely happy story when pulling Tarot cards and you have the Tower card or Ten of Swords. Likewise it's hard to feel sorry for yourself when your reading is dominated by the Sun card, Ten of Discs and Six of Wands. The fixed systems are also established language systems that the universe, divinity or your higher self can use to get a message through to you. It's like an agreed upon code that you both have access to use and understand. But on the downside, the systems require greater knowledge, and they are limited by the symbols within them. You might need to look up an answer to a system, but ideally, if the universal intelligence guided you to it, the answer in the book you have handy will probably have a message for you.

Fluid systems give more flexibility, but can be hard to read, especially for yourself, because no training covers all possibilities. You have to be more intuitive and go with the flow. Being in a meditative state, receptive to the universal force speaking to you through these symbols, is even more critical. The answers are not as handy as a simple guidebook of interpretation. Much like dreams, they are subjective, based upon both universal and mythic symbolism, and those of a specific culture, time period and even person. What one symbol might mean to you, even with a great education in mysticism, might mean something totally different to another practitioner with a slightly different education. Sometimes seeking the advice of others on these interpretations is helpful, and other times, very confusing.

Good magicians perform divinations regularly. The purpose can range from seeking advice on what to do next or what any given day will hold and how to best prepare for it. Those who are focused on the magickal life and seek their True Will do so to attune better to their True Will, and see the information as coming from the Soul or Higher Self, the higher, wiser part of them.

Before doing any spellcraft, it is good to ask this part of yourself, through a divination system, ideally a fixed oracle device, if you should. If the omen is bad, rethink your spell or wait for another time. The omens might be bad because it is simply a bad time to do this and be successful. Cosmically, the forces of the Moon, planets and stars might be against you, as if you were swimming upstream, or it might simply be a harmful intention in regard to your True Will. At best it's a waste of energy that won't manifest. At worst it will manifest something that might ultimately bring you a lesson, but be unpleasant, and if you asked, unnecessary. The divination can help you understand the lesson and avoid the waste of energy. Sometimes the omen is bad because what you have planned is not the best way to go about the situation, and the omen can give you additional insight on the best intention. When you change it and pull a card or symbol for another omen, it can then be positive and you should go forward.

I highly recommend learning an oracle system of fixed symbols as well as the art of a more fluid system. I personally prefer the Tarot and the dark mirror and have spent a lot of time in the study and practice of both. Performing a simple oracle pull daily is ideal, particularly when learning. At the start of your day ask what you need to know and pull one to three symbols. What does it tell you and does your day match up? For the skeptics, pull them and keep them face down until the evening, then see if your day matches up with the symbols that were unknown to you during the day, but waiting on your altar or other special magickal space.

While self-divinations are important, I also recommend receiving a reading from a practitioner who is not involved in your daily life regularly, perhaps once a year. They can give you insight and information from the divine, acting as a translator in your magickal conversation with the universe, giving you messages you might not want to hear or be able to understand otherwise. Most metaphysical communities have reputable psychics and divination experts. Seek them out as needed.

Exercise: Divination

As you develop your magickal skills, also seek to educate yourself on a divinatory art. Pick one that calls to you and draw from it daily to learn the meanings and familiarize yourself with how it works.

Developing both meditation and divination will balance out your magickal conversation and the skills of spell casting focused upon in this book. They can be a great aid in answering a lot of your own questions on your spellcraft, including when to do it and when not to do it.

Chapter Three: The Three Requirements of Magick

All magick, at least all magick with a result in mind, requires three basic things: Intention, Will, and Energy. With all three, your spell has the most likely chance of succeeding. When you are missing any one of them, you are likely to fail. They are the necessary basic components for the making of magick. Each is quite simple, yet profound. When you understand how to harness them, your magick takes an amazing leap. Many traditions of magick unconsciously harness them through their techniques and tools, but a direct understanding can help you when you craft your own magick and rituals.

Intention

Intention is the seed of all spellcraft, and in fact, all magickal life. Just as magick is a conversation that involves speaking and listening, magick is a delicate balance between intention and acceptance. You must have an intention, a desire, and an outcome in mind before you can cast a spell.

I had a healing teacher who said intention is the seed of all development, and intention rules everything. Your intention is the most important thing, as it's the impetus of all that follows in your life. It overrules everything else. While I agree with the sentiment, there is one thing more important than intention – clear intention.

Many people have confused intentions, vague and unknowing. They have a general sense of wanting to be happy or successful, and no clear understanding of what exactly will make them happy or successful. Clear intention is necessary for a successful spell. You must know what you are creating to actually create it. Even if you simply want to be happy and understand what happiness is to you, then that is a clear intention. But if you have no idea what being happy would be like, then your intention is not quite clear and the potential for mis-spellings is ripe.

Before doing any spell, ask yourself, "How would my life be different right now if this spell is successful?" How would you feel – emotionally, mentally and physically? What conditions would be different? Imagine a day in your life after the spell is successful, from waking up to going to bed. What is different on all levels? If you can answer these questions, you have a clear intention.

When forming your intention, it is always best to focus your spell on the end result. What is the final result that you want to create? Do not focus on the method of arrival. There can be many methods where the same result can come to you, and if you focus on one only, you close the door of possibilities to those other avenues of manifestation.

For example, you want to go on vacation to Hawaii. If you do a spell for the money to go on vacation, that is the method by which you might get there, not the end result. The end result is the vacation. You could also win a vacation in a contest, be asked by an affluent friend to come for free, or suddenly find you have business that requires you to go to Hawaii and have the opportunity to stay longer for fun on your company's expense account. Any of those would be acceptable to fulfill your intention of a vacation in Hawaii, but if you just fixated on the money, you close these other doors to manifestation.

In forming your clear intention, you can add stipulations, and will learn to do so when writing petition spells with conditions, but they are all part of the end results. A simple stipulation that it is acceptable to me, harms none, or is for the highest good, prevents your magick from killing a relative who bequeaths the money to you in their will, or from getting into an accident yourself with money from the settlement to fund your vacation. That would not be acceptable, for the highest good, or harming none.

You can also stipulate you want to be on the island of Maui instead of Oahu, or go for seven days. They all add to the clear intention. Find the balance point between a clear, simple intention and a level of specificity that makes the spell too complex and hard to manifest. That helps you get down to what is really important and what is not. Ultimately, in this example, the vacation, the relaxation, and the fun are important. If you get hung up on it having to be a specific hotel, on a specific floor, and in the corner suite, the amount of conditions might make the spell almost impossible to produce. Learning this is the balance point between intention and acceptance.

Exercise: Visualize Success

Whenever doing any spellcraft, I find an important question to answer to clarify my intention is, "How will my life be different when this spell succeeds?" How will it tangibly and quantifiably be different? Imagine going through your next day as if the spell were a total success. From getting up in the morning to going to bed, what would you be doing differently? Where would you be? How would you feel? Is there any noticeable difference? If the answer is "no," or "I don't know," your intention is probably not very clear and you need to refine it before you do any spell crafting.

Will

Will is the second component to spell casting. Not only do you have to be clear about what you want, you also have to have the drive, the desire, to actually create it. As we learned from Mr. Crowley, "will" (and "Will") can mean a lot of different things. On the first level, it is strength of will. Is your drive sufficient to fuel your intention? Will is like the spark that ignites the fuse of your magick. If your drive doesn't have enough spark to it, the fuse is never lit.

This is one of the reasons why it is hard to do magick for someone else. We usually don't want things sufficiently for other people in the way we do for ourselves. In magick, will relates to the element of fire, our life force and energy. Fire is defined by some as the quest for identity. Where do you put your life force? That is where you discover who you are in this world. We call the Western Mystery traditions the "Great Work" implying you are here to do something with your life. Like the master temple builders of Sumer and Egypt, you are here to craft, to build, your spiritual life. Your will, with passion and desire, is what leads you, just like an artist, to that creation.

Working for others is not about your identity, your passion and life force, so it's harder. Professional spell casters either have learned techniques to stoke their emotional fervor to generate such will for another, or simply compile the spell materials and insist the recipient metaphorically or literally light the fuse. The action of using the spell components, carrying a charm, reciting a prayer or lighting a candle, engages the recipient's will in the matter. If they don't want it, the spell consultant is not to blame.

Beyond the drive and desire for the intention, "will" also refers to the True Will. Desire and the personal will for something leads us to True Will if we do our magick in accord with seeking our True Will. That which works for us obviously has sufficient will, for True Will trumps personal will every time. If we do spells for something with any of our "highest good" stipulations, and our True Will is out of alignment with the intention, then the spell will not work, because sufficient will is not there. In fact, the True Will is

The Casting of Spells

conflicting against it, so there is no real life force to back it up, even if we think there is. What we confuse for will in those situations is a complex of confusion. We confused something that is actually not good for us for something that is, and our magick can lead us in a direction to untangle and understand that complex, freeing the energy trapped in it for other things on our path of magickal evolution. This is not to say that short term harmful magick to yourself and others is not real, but it carries none of the stipulation or intention of highest Will. The conflict with higher Will leads to either change or destruction.

Exercise: Divination of True Will

Go back to your written answer about True Will. Now perform a divination on that answer, asking if in this moment, that answer is the most correct for you. What does your divination reveal? Are you mostly on target, or does the divination show your conscious perception of your True Will and your actual True Will are miles apart? If the latter, you'll have personal transformative work to do as you craft your magick. The things that work best will lead you to True Will. The ones that don't work need to be examined. Was it faulty spellcraft? Was your timing for your intention against the tides of life? Was the intention unclear or mis-worded? Do you have psychological, energetic, or spiritual blocks to the success of the spell that need to be worked out? Or does the desire itself conflict with your True Will, so that your desire needs to be examined and transformed in light of self-sabotaging patterns? All are important questions to ask and explore when our magick fails.

Energy

Energy is the third and final component, and it is often confused with will. Isn't will connected to life force, and life force to energy? Yes, but for this third component, energy refers to both the potential energy to fuel it and the method to direct it. Will lights the fuse, but if the fuse is not connected to anything, nothing happens. A fuse connected to a bomb filled with gunpowder, or a fireworks rocket, will have a more spectacular and tangible result than just a fuse alone.

The source of the energy, the potential power to manifest, like the gunpowder, explosive or rocket fuel of our fuse analogy, can come in many different forms. Individual spell casters, and specific traditions and techniques of magick can favor one source over another, but basically they all fall into four main categories:

Personal – Personal energy is the energy contained within your body and your personal energy field, your aura. It is the energy of your body, from the thermal heat of your metabolism to the subtle life force flowing through your etheric anatomy and around your aura. Your thoughts and emotions are a part of your personal energy. Strong intention, will and emotion can be sufficient to fuel a spell. Many people who are not versed in magick or prayer, but are simply powerful personalities, have learned to stoke their life force through emotion and ambition and apply it in ways we could consider magickal for their own personal goals and success. You see this in business, art and entertainment.

Terrestrial – Terrestrial energy, also known as Telluric Energy, is the power found within the Earth, the land and nature. Just as our bodies are filled with life force, so too, is the body of the Earth. Certain places are known as power spots in ancient traditions, and magick done there can be particularly effective. Mountains, shores, groves and swamps all have their own power. Spell casters aware of energy draw it up from the Earth to fuel their spell casting. Other traditions draw items out of nature, and use their inherent energies. Magick involving stones, wood, herbs, animals or water are tapping into the terrestrial energies that these items have absorbed and shaped in specific ways.

Celestial – Celestial energy is the power of the sky, including the Sun, Moon, planets and stars. Vast systems of magick involving the timing of magick to astrological phenomena are quite common all around the world. Such rituals are drawing upon the energy of favorable alignments. These alignments can also be corresponded with items from the Earth to use as spell ingredients. Magicians can draw down the energy of the sky or specific celestial bodies to fuel their spells.

Divine – Divine energy can be a catchall phrase for anything not involved in the other three forms of energy, which technically, from a religious point of view, could all be considered divine as part of creation. Divine energy specifically refers to drawing upon the energy of the universe as a divinity, a specific divinity from a cultural mythos, or another entity or spirit – an angel, demon, djinn, faery, elemental (although they can be considered terrestrial energies as well), ancestor or even ghost. If an entity is lending its energy to the spell intention, it is considered divine. Even some forms of sacred language, mantras invoking an aspect of creation or specific divinity, are a way of generating divine energy through the interface of personal energy, as we are the ones doing the chanting.

Exercise: Drawing Energy

Stand tall with your feet firmly planted on the floor, just wider than your shoulders. Close your eyes. Breathe deeply. Relax your body. Relax your mind. Open yourself up to the magickal possibilities.

As you inhale, imagine that you are inhaling from the soles of your feet. You draw up heat or vibrations from the land beneath you, like air, and into your feet and legs. As you breathe, you draw it up from the legs and into the belly. From the belly, into the heart and chest. Feel it circulate within you.

As you inhale, imagine that you are now inhaling from the crown of your head. Draw down the heat or vibrations into your head, neck, shoulders, arms and chest. Feel it circulate within you, mixing with the energy from below.

As you inhale, draw energy from both below and above, mixing them together, and as you exhale, radiate them out from your heart in all directions, like the light of a small sun. Feel their power warm and heal all the cells in your body, and extend arm's length all around you.

When you exhale, you can also imagine you are exhaling through the palms of your hands, directing the energy with your hands, or beaming it in a straight line out of your heart or brow.

Experiment and explore. When done, let the remaining energy fall back down into the Earth. Place your hands on the floor and imagine pushing out the excess, grounding it into the Earth. If you feel lightheaded, have some food and do something "normal" to ground yourself into normal conscious awareness.

Methods of energy direction vary according to the type of energy, the practitioner and the tradition. These techniques can be simple intention and visualizations, reciting words of power, ritual gestures, directed breath, spoken words, burning items, making offerings, the creation and consecration of charms, or more complex rituals combining many of these techniques. These techniques gather the energy, imprint it with intention and will, and direct it towards its goal. Without a proven method to direct energy towards your spell's result, you are simply daydreaming of your intention, not practicing magick. This final component is a key that many unsuccessful magicians do not understand, and thereby are ineffective. To be a successful magician, we must learn to not only be in touch with these three essentials, but effectively line them up together in unison for our spell.

Chapter Four: Trance Techniques

Trance techniques in magick are vitally important, yet so subtle that many books on the subject overlook them completely. That's because many of the rituals themselves done in spellcrafting are a subtle technology to induce trance and project the energy of your intention out into the universe for manifestation. They aren't emphasized as a technique because they become part of the mystique of the spell. That's why many people erroneously believe the spell itself really has all the power, when in fact the spell caster is the one fueling the results of the spell. The ritual procedures open the channel and allow access to a variety of energies, but without the spell caster they would be nothing. Sadly, movie magick overemphasizes the power of the spell itself, so people think it's like chemistry. If you simply mix the right things together or say the appropriate words, poof, your spell is guaranteed. This view discounts the need for clear intention, will, and energy direction, and the process that aligns all three of these requirements is trance.

Brain Waves

Trance is the method whereby we make that ever elusive change in consciousness. Technically, when we define magick as a change of consciousness, we are usually referring to a change of perception about a particular fact or phenomenon, such as a change in your thoughts and feelings about money, love or illness. Yet those are all fairly unquantifiable, at least by science. But trance literally changes your consciousness, your brain wave patterns.

Normal consciousness is defined by science as the Beta brain wave state. You are awake, aware, alert and working. Beta is 13 to 16 cycles per second, or hertz. Alpha, just below Beta, is defined as 8 to 13 Hz, but indicates a creativity, fluidity and daydream-like quality. Inspiration, intuition and psychic phenomena are more likely at this brain wave state. We often have distorted perceptions of time and space, and lose focus on the here and now to tune into other perceptions and realities. Below Alpha, at 4 to 9 Hz is Theta, where we have deeper states of trance and visionary journey, and there is even one state below Theta. Delta is the deepest level of trance, and the deepest level of sleep. It's no thoughts and almost no activity, at 1 to 4 Hz.

Trance techniques move you from Beta into these lower forms of consciousness. Lower is not necessarily bad and higher better, but lower here means slower, deeper and otherworldly. Sometimes we mistake higher for always being better in our modern metaphysical society, but in terms of brain waves in magick and meditation, lower is preferable. Think of it simply as deeper.

A trance technique may be calming, often defined as inhibitory, as it inhibits and slows body systems, or exhibitory, as it excites body systems. They both serve to lower the brain waves. Even the excited body action in trance technique is repetitive, and the repetitive state entrains the brain waves, like a group of windup clocks all ticking together, until they take on the dominant clock pattern. In that entrainment, the brain waves are lowered to the dominant frequency.

Meditative (Inhibitory) Techniques

Hypnotic Induction – While hypnosis has gotten a bad reputation among some, the concept of using suggestions from another or upon yourself to enter a trance state is simple, fast and effective. Simply counting backwards from twelve to one with your eyes closed can bring you into an altered state.

Repetitive Action – Focusing upon any repetitive action done in a slow rhythm puts you into a meditative state. Focusing upon, or simply counting, your breaths is a great technique. You can count the number of breaths, or count in a pattern. A simple form of breath work involves counting to the number four as you inhale, holding for the count of four, exhaling to the count of four, and holding the breath out for the count of four, then repeating. Any internal mantra, a word or series of words, with meanings known or unknown, can induce trance. A simple technique is repeating your name over and over again, silently within, or softly out loud. Any slow movement will also induce trance, such as slow, regular walking, rocking back and forth, or tapping your foot.

Formal Ritual – The actions of most formal rituals are repetitive and precise, the actions that help induce trance.

Fasting – Abstaining from food for a time can help induce trance, usually once you get over the period of thinking about being hungry. Various fasting diets, on water, herbal teas, broths and juices can also induce trance. Avoiding heavy foods, particularly starches, meats, and bottom-feeding ocean dwellers, can help facilitate trance.

Sleep – Sleep is a form of trance that everyone gets into regularly for general health and rest. Learning to be lucid in the dream state is a powerful yet difficult form of trance.

Isolation – Removing yourself from outside stimuli, be it electronic or spoken communication, people, technology, and even light, induces trance. Spending time in the traditional cave or mountain top is a type of isolation, but so is a dark room with no noise.

Ecstatic (Exhibitory) Techniques

Repetitive Action – Exhibitory repetitive actions include playing or listening to a rhythm instrument, such as a drum, rattle or even crystal bowl, and dancing, rhythmic shaking or jumping.

Sex – Sex induces an altered state of awareness, be it alone, with a partner or in a group. The sensations of sexual activity, and the rhythms and tides to it, definitely alter perceptions.

Pain – Not so different from sex on a biological level, the sensations of regular and rhythmic pain, from ritual flagellation to getting a tattoo, help induce altered perceptions and awareness.

Intoxication – Intoxication on a magickal level can refer to alcohol, but also to other sacraments ranging from oils and incense that help relax or excite the body or to entheogenic sacraments that transform brain chemistry to produce major shifts in awareness, such as psilocybin mushrooms, peyote or datura.

Setting – Setting, like intoxication, can technically be inhibitory or exhibitory, depending on the circumstances. The location and specifically the land, can help induce an altered state. Liminal locations where two different things meet are helpful for trance – crossroads, graveyards, seashore, swamp, hedge and mountaintop. Timing of the day, season or astrology can help induce altered awareness. Sunrise/sunset, equinoxes/solstices and various Moon signs can aid magick and trance.

Clothing – Magickal vestments, garments, jewelry, or lack thereof, can help induce a new perspective. If you wear something you only wear for ritual and trance magick, then putting it on sends a subtle signal to your consciousness, like a Pavlovian response, to change to the appropriate setting for the work. It does take time to program the response through repeated use of the article in question.

Exercise: Inducing Trance

Pick a safe inhibitory and exhibitory technique to explore and try it several times. When done each session, evaluate how you felt during it. Do you feel you effectively reached a trance state? You might find good trance is often subtle, no different than daydreaming or letting your mind wander, except you have greater awareness and control, as you have consciously willed the trance state.

In a class on spell casting, a very inquisitive woman asked me why we had to alter our consciousness. Why did we have to enter trance? Why didn't the spell just work without it? Think of the times you are in Beta consciousness. You cannot perceive a magickal reality. It's all about the business of the "real" world, at least what is real to most other people. If you can't perceive magick, how can you work with it, cast it and make it do what you want to do? Most of your magickal experiences take place in states of lower brain wave activity. If that is where you experience the magickal and psychic, then that is where you can create it. Otherwise, your rational mind, dominant in Beta brain wave state, short-circuits the ritual. Your logical mind cannot experience the temporary suspension of disbelief to get the magick done. So in truth, Dion Fortune was right when she focused on the change of magick to be "in consciousness." If you don't know the art of altering consciousness in this most fundamental way, you won't be able to make long-term and permanent adaptations to your condition and transform your life.

Chapter Five: Techniques of Spellcasting

To cast a spell, you need a technique. That is the key, as the technique is ultimately the mechanism for you to direct energy. The ritual of the spell can help you focus your intention and gather your will, but often those are already set before you begin. Spells are methods to direct and release energy for manifestation.

Many of the effective spell techniques are considered traditional, passed on in similar forms in many cultures because they are effective. Some of the most basic techniques found the world over include:

Direct Petition – A petition is a direct request to divinity/spirit/universe, usually written down, or sometimes spoken. Out of all the magickal techniques, it is closest to a prayer or a supplication. Though all spells are often described as focused prayer to the layman, they technically are not unless they are similar to petitions. Petition spells align your personal intention and will with divine energy and divine Will.

Incantation – An incantation is a spoken spell, consisting of words of clear intention or words of power. It's sometimes known as a charm, in the sense one can charm another by speaking physically, or a rune, in the sense of a verse. (In other traditions of magick, a charm can mean a talisman or amulet and a rune can be a specific type of symbol from Norse and Saxon traditions.) Often incantations are spoken in verse with trance inducing rhyme and meter. The process of speaking the incantation evokes the magick, and aligns you with the energies conjured by the words. When using foreign words of power, the words are often methods of summoning specific energies, like chanting the Norse runes, Sanskrit mantras or Hebrew names of God.

Correspondence – Correspondence works on the principle of "As above, so below." Patterns repeat themselves endlessly if one knows where to look. Correspondence magick uses various items from nature that contain terrestrial power, such as herbs, woods, stones, metals and wax. They have an inherent quality or characteristic that corresponds their energy to an abstract intention in the human realm, such as love, money, or protection. Correspondence magick can also mean to time the spell with various planetary or stellar alignments to infuse the work with celestial energy. Many magicians will combine the two techniques, as there is also a correspondence between the planets, stars, and even the days of the week with natural substances used in magick. The item provides the physical anchor for the phenomenon in the sky. Ritually empowering it and carrying it with you can bring that fortunate influence with you wherever you go, even when the astrological alignment has passed.

Contagion – The magickal Law of Contagion states that once two things have touched, on an energetic or astral level, they are always touching. The word has the same root as contagious. One can transfer to another like an illness can be passed, but the magick of contagion does not have to be harmful like an illness. Contagion spells require an item from the target or recipient of the magick, often called a "tag-lock." Anything the intended recipient has touched is suitable, though more intimate items are stronger links. Clothing, a handkerchief, a piece of well-worn jewelry or anything with bodily fluids or genetic material—hair, nail clippings, blood, or sexual fluids—makes a powerful link. Contagion rituals align your intention, will, and energy with the target. Ritual actions done to the object are thereby directed energetically to the recipient. A common form of contagion magick is to make a poppet out of the recipient's clothing, the stereotypical voodoo doll—which actually originally comes from European, not African, magick—and what you do to the doll is done to the person. While movies and novels often show only harm, the same poppet can be used with the intention of healing and blessing.

Symbol – Symbol magick uses a similar principle to contagion, but rather than the two objects having touched, one object can be a symbol, a representation, of the recipient, such as a photo that the recipient never touched (if the recipient handled the photo it is also contagion) or a symbol that evokes another magickal power for the spell. If you make a poppet out of material that the recipient hasn't touched, it would technically not be contagion magick, but symbol magick. The doll is considered an effigy. Cloth, wax, and clay effigies are popular and easy to make. Various ancient and modern sigils, runes, glyphs, pentacles, amulets, and mandalas are forms of symbol magick. Various grimoires are filled with symbols to align with specific angels, djinn, gods, elementals, and planetary spirits to conjure specific magickal effects.

Ritual – A full ritual will involve many of the techniques above coupled with greater physical actions. Formal ritual is the big gun of spell casting techniques, as it combines several smaller techniques into one focused event. Technically all the smaller techniques are rituals as well, but when we list ritual as a technique, we mean more intricate, prescribed actions done for a common purpose. Ritual is often akin to yoga in the Western traditions, as the ritual movements are designed to generate, or connect us to, magickal forces that aid in our process of evolution and enlightenment. They connect us to forces seemingly outside of our body and consciousness, the terrestrial, celestial and divine energy, as well as kindle, focus and direct our personal energy.

Physical action is necessary or at the very least more helpful, to create a physical change in the world. The actions and forces they connect us to also help fuel our spells. Rituals set the space, creating what is known as a sacred space, a place of clearer and more focused communion with the divine and all of creation. Rituals such as the Magick Circle, or any elementally based ritual, directly connects us to the forces of creation as embodied by the elements, making our magick that much more powerful.

Magickal techniques such as correspondence, contagion, symbol, and the strongly written or spoken word help put us into the correct frame of consciousness. Going back to Dion Fortune's definition of magick, "change in consciousness," these tools and techniques help us change our consciousness, even for a moment, by providing the right framework and setting to truly believe in the change we want to create, enough so to make it real in that moment. If the spell is cast in that moment, then success is possible, even in areas of your life that you are normally depressed about and can't otherwise conceive of success.

Magick seems to put us into a no-win, Catch-22 situation. We are told that unless we truly feel love, we won't successfully cast a love spell. But if we feel love, then we probably have a loving relationship and wouldn't need it. We can't cast a successful prosperity spell until we feel worthy of it, that we are prosperous and deserving. Again, when we are poor and the rent is due, how do we feel rich? With magickal technique and, in particular, correspondence. Technically, words spoken and written, symbols and signs and objects that have touched each other, along with the items of nature and celestial phenomenon, all have the correspondence principle behind them.

A good way of looking at the principle is through the magickal Law of Octaves, or to simply think of the universe as a grand piano. On the piano, the pattern of seven white keys and five black keys repeats. Each repetition of the same notes, higher or lower, is an octave. If you hold the pedal down on the piano and strike any note, the corresponding notes in the other octaves will also ring. Hit Middle C and all the C's will vibrate on a true piano. We're not talking about electronic keyboards here, but strings and tiny keyboard hammers.

Now imagine that some of those octaves are in your reach. Others are literally out of your reach, and too high or too low to effectively hear. The ones in your reach are like the tools you have access to on planet Earth. The ones out of your reach are metaphysical principles and forces of the universe you can't touch, hold onto or point to, but they are just as real to you. They are things like love, prosperity, protection, healing, attraction, inspiration, beauty, and creation.

If you want to strike the note of love, and you think you know where it is, but it's so high up you can't reach it, correspondence and ritual can help you do that. You can perform the ritual on Friday, the day of Venus. You can wait till the Moon is in Taurus or Libra, the signs of Venus and conducive to love. You can wear copper jewelry, the metal of Venus. You can chant Inanna, Ishtar, Astarte, Aphrodite, Venus, Hathor over and over again, goddesses all associated with love. Sing it on the literal note F or in the key of F. Write out your wish on pink paper with Dove's Blood Ink (an herbal formula) or green Venusian ink. You can burn red sandalwood incense. Wear rose oil. Drink Lady's Mantle tea as a part of the ritual. You can draw the glyph of Venus or the Norse rune Kenaz in the four directions around you. Visualize doves. Wear green. Carry a rose quartz or emerald in your pocket.

All of these things will generate a similar energy, a similar vibration, corresponding to love. Each one is like striking the corresponding note for love on the lower octaves within your reach on the piano. The high note of love, out of reach, will ring without you even touching it. You will "hear" and "feel" love during the ritual, and if you cast your spell then, you'll be casting it from a "change in consciousness" even temporarily and have success.

While this book focuses on written petitions and spoken incantations, but not correspondences, understanding the principles of magick will help you as you add and develop more techniques to your magickal tool box.

The Elements

The elements are considered to be the four fundamental forces of the universe. While we use terrestrial phenomena to represent them, the energies of the elements really embody forces of creation and destruction that sustain our universe. Earth is not just rocks, stones and soil, but the principle of physicality. Water is not just H_2O, but the principle of shape and form, described by occultists as the astral. It is most influenced by our emotions and dreams. Air is not just the gases of the atmosphere, the winds and breezes, but the principle of idea, language and structure. Fire is not just combustion, but the quality of energy, vitality, passion and life force. Fire is the individual spark.

In people, fire, air, water, and earth are akin to the soul, mind, heart, and body. Others correspond them to the scientific principles of electromagnetism, strong nuclear force, weak nuclear force, and gravity. In biology, they are the building blocks of DNA – A-G-C-T. In esoteric principle, they are connected with four "L" words to express their highest principles – Light, Life, Love, and Law. Others relate them to the words Destiny or Will, Truth, Compassion, and Sovereignty, respectively.

In magick, fire is the impetus, the idea, the personal will that can lead to True Will. Air is like the blueprint that will shape the astral water that takes form. It is the language and structure of the intent, beyond the impetus to create or change. Water is the pattern formed, the container for the energy, the shape, fueled by strong emotions channeled during ritual. Earth is the manifestation of the spell. It is said anything created on the astral and instilled with energy, precipitates down into the physical at some point, unless you rob it of its energy to manifest. Spell work reaches up through the elements to Fire, or even beyond to Spirit, when doing work for the Highest Good and in accord with True will, and then draws the energy down this ladder, precipitating the intention from the highest level down into full tangible manifestation.

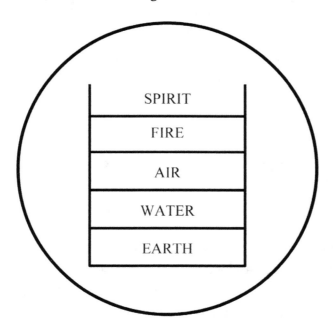

Elemental Ladder

Each of the five senses is associated with the elements, the four plus spirit. The pentacle represents the five senses, plus the circle as the mysterious sixth sense of psychic ability around the five pointed star. Rituals that stimulate a sense help activate and kindle that elemental power within us to fuel our magick. Some of the best rituals use all of the senses to make magickal connections.

SPIRIT
HEARING

AIR
SMELL

WATER
TASTE

EARTH
TOUCH

FIRE
SIGHT

Pentacle with the Senses/Elements

If you've ever attended a ritual, from a Witch's Sabbat to a High Catholic Mass, you can look at the list and see how many of the senses are stimulated. Colored candles and colored vestments are used. The air is perfumed with flowers, incense, or anointing oil, setting the magickal atmosphere. Ritual sacraments of cakes,

The Casting of Spells

bread, water, wine or herbs are used. One is touched at some point, with ritual gestures, anointing with water, shaking or holding hands. Intentions are spoken aloud, and something may be said in a foreign language that helps induce trance. These are the technological nuts and bolts of a good ritual, making ritual a form of magickal technology.

Element	Sense	Magickal Connections
Fire	Sight	Light, fire, color, symbols and inner visualization.
Air	Smell	Scented oil, perfume, incense, burning wood, herbs and fresh flowers.
Water	Taste	Water, wine, potions, elixirs, breads, cakes and other ritual sacraments.
Earth	Touch	Anointing with potions, hand holding, touch, sexual contact, barefoot.
Spirit	Hearing	Spoken words, chants, songs, bells, drums and all instruments.

Magick Circle Technique

The magick circle is the standard ritual of Witches and magicians. Until the rise of the Golden Dawn tradition, and later the advent of modern Wicca, there were no set and prescribed forms of the magick circle. Practitioners did them all their own way, yet we can look at ancient art, medieval wood cuts, and surviving grimoires and spells to see how many of the occult traditions drew, traced, walked, danced or otherwise marked a circle as their ritual space. They were imitating the image of the heavens, the circle of the Sun or Moon upon the Earth, and standing in that powerful place.

Typically, but not always, they would honor the four directions. In modern western occultism, the four directions are associated with the four classic elements, with the fifth in the center. You see similar techniques, with slightly different meanings and words, in tribal practices from across the world, and in particular, in Native American Medicine Circle rituals from both North and South America.

Woodcut of the Ritual Circle

My own experiences of the magick circle are through the traditions of Wicca and Witchcraft, and my own understanding

The Casting of Spells

comes from that foundation. The example I'll give here will be teaching it from that perspective, without the religious aspects from practicing the religion of Wicca. You can use this technique in any context. I look at it as a magickal technology, available to anyone, like fire, electricity, fermentation, or the wheel. It is just slightly more esoteric.

To begin with, ideally you would have a magickal wand or a ritual blade to create the space. A piece of wood from nature you feel a connection to can serve as a magick wand. Those in religious traditions have specific instructions on how to obtain the wand, what its meaning and responsibilities are, and how to care for it, but if you are using it for strictly functional purposes, any one that you feel a connection with will do.

You can also set up a simple altar. While "altar" implies a religious ceremony, for these purposes an altar is really a magickal work-space. It's a station where you perform your spells and can leave out any material components to keep a long term spell "going." Along with the wand, which is technically a tool of fire, or the blade, which is of air, you can have representatives of the four elements on your altar space, set up in the four directions. A stone, crystal or bowl of salt is good for earth. A ritual pentacle, known as a peyton or paten, is also a symbol of earth, as well as all five elements. A cup or bowl of water, or a sea shell is a tool of water. Traditionally for Witches it is a silver chalice. Incense is an appropriate tool of air, though also the ritual blade known as an athame, double-edged with a dark handle, is also a tool of air. And the candle can be an additional tool of fire. For spirit, a larger flameproof vessel, suitable for burning petition spells, is ideal. I use an old-fashioned iron cauldron.

Altar

The magick circle is best done in a state of very light trance –
enough to alter consciousness but not so deep that you can't move
or light candles and speak words. It is considered to be a state of
Alpha, or ritual consciousness. The basics of a nonreligious circle,
at least as I do it, can be divided into the following steps:

Cleansing – Cleansing refers to clearing yourself and the space
before actually doing any magick or ritual. You can cleanse
yourself physically and psychically with a simple shower or bath.
Traditionally, baths have salt and oils in them, such as lavender,
lemon or hyssop. You can cleanse your space by burning a
purifying incense or herb in the space, such as sage, or a mixture of
sage, cedar and sweet grass, frankincense, or a blend of
frankincense and myrrh, lavender, cinnamon, or pine. Often loose
incense is burned upon a charcoal disc within a heat proof
container. These can be found in metaphysical supply shops. For
those adverse to smoke, a spray bottle with 50% water to 50%

The Casting of Spells

alcohol, plus a few drops of any of these herbs alone or in combination in essential oil form, can be spritzed around the room for cleansing the psychic space.

Centering – Centering simply refers to gathering your energy and awareness and focusing it in preparation for magick. Feeling your feet firmly on the floor and taking a few deep breaths and focusing on the intention of ritual is enough to center yourself for the task. Rushing into something without proper focus, scattered in energy and intention, is the opposite of being centered.

Casting Circle – Take your wand or blade, holding it just above head level and starting in the north, and envision the tip creating a line of bright blue colored light as you trace the circumference of the ritual space as a perfect circle clockwise, or deosil ("sun-wise"). Even if you can't move in a perfect circle, envision it as perfect. Trace it three times, saying these or similar words:

I cast this circle to protect me from all that may come to do me harm.

I charge this circle to draw in the most perfect energies to my work.

I create a space beyond space and a time beyond time, a Temple of Magick where all is possible.

So mote it be.

When done, you might find the circle becomes more like a sphere around you.

Calling Quarters – Calling the quarters invites the energies of the four primal elements. Face each direction, holding out your hands, and say:

To the North, I call upon the spirits of the element of Earth to aid me in my magick.

Hail and welcome.

To the East, I call upon the spirits of the element of Fire to aid me in my magick.

Hail and welcome.

To the South, I call upon the spirits of the element of Air to aid me in my magick.

Hail and welcome.

To the West, I call upon the spirits of the element of Water to aid me in my magick.

Hail and welcome.

Evoking Divinity – Invite the divine powers, your partners in the magickal conversation, to join you in the sacred space. Even if you envision this power as ever present, a ritual invitation establishes a stronger connection. From my own practices, I say:

I call upon the Goddess, God, and Great Spirit to be here with me.

Hail and welcome.

Naming the Work – Simply state the purpose of the ritual, to focus the intent. For example:

I create this sacred space to cast a spell of prosperity and good fortune.

Proper Protection – An additional optional step is to anoint yourself with a protection potion of some sort, or simply a mixture of water and salt, to ensure you are clear of anything that you might have brought into the circle space before doing magick.

I anoint myself with this protection potion, to protect me from all harm on any level.

So mote it be.

The Work – Perform your spellcraft, divination or meditation in the center of the circle.

Devoking Divinity – Acknowledge the end of the working time and space with your divine partner.

I thank and release the Goddess, God, and Great Spirit from this space.

Stay if you will, go if you must.

Hail and farewell.

Release the Quarters – Release the powers of the four quarters, facing them and moving counterclockwise or widdershins ("against the sun").

To the North, I thank and release the spirits of the element of Earth.

Hail and farewell.

To the West, I thank and release the spirits of the element of Water.

Hail and farewell.

To the South, I thank and release the spirits of the element of Air.

Hail and farewell.

To the East, I thank and release the spirits of the element of Fire.

Hail and farewell.

Release the Circle – Take your circle casting tool and face the north, moving counterclockwise or widdershins and ending in the north again. Imagine either infinitely expanding the circle/sphere or sucking it back up into the tool.

Please note that since deosil is sun-wise and widdershins is "against the sun," they are reversed in the southern hemisphere: counterclockwise for deosil/casting and clockwise for widdershins/releasing.

I cast this circle out into the cosmos as a sign of my work. The circle is undone, but never broken.

So mote it be.

Grounding – Make sure your awareness has returned to normal. Touch the Earth/floor and imagine releasing any excess magickal charge, as if you had a grounding wire releasing an excess electric charge. You can stamp your foot, clap your hands or eat some food to help bring your awareness to the physical realm.

I find that any spellcraft done in a magick circle is ultimately more powerful than any other work I've done, but that is coming from the perspective of a Witchcraft priest. You might feel differently and want to keep things simple. But this technique can be very helpful as you expand beyond petition work into other forms of magick outlined by future volumes of this series.

For those looking for more of the theology and philosophy behind the magick circle, I suggest my book, *The Outer Temple of Witchcraft: Circles, Spells and Rituals.*

Chapter Six: The Tides of the Moon and Sun

The Moon and Sun are said to have a tremendous influence over life on Earth, and any observant spell caster would agree. On a physical level, it's obvious how the Sun influences life. Without it, weather, atmosphere and photosynthesis would affect life very differently for humanity. The Moon pulls on the tides of the ocean and the water within our bodies, influencing more subtle yet important cycles. The stars and space which the Sun and Moon seem to occupy indicate, if not cause, the seasonal changes, as the planet changes locations over the year, and subtly shifts over thousands of years. Our relationship to the stars changes the stories we tell ourselves as a people.

On a more etheric or astral level, the influence of the heavens can certainly be felt, even if you don't perceive the source. The art and science of astrology, based upon the principle of correspondence, "As above, so below," is the foundation of it. The patterns on the Earth are reflected in the sky and vice versa. The sky gives us a wider perspective to see our own lives, and when it comes to spell casting, can help us understand when the best time to initiate a project is and when to avoid it. Ancient people would consult astrologers for the most fortunate time to build a temple, plant the crops or crown a king. Today, many of the subtly wise consult astrologers on marriage, finance, and other major decisions. Magick can be considered the first project, the first intention, to any tangible result we want to create.

While astrology is a vast topic in itself, modern spell casters first learn to focus on the Moon and the Sun as the visibly largest and most dominant celestial bodies. Though we know the Sun dwarfs the Moon in terms of actual size, in our perception, they are roughly the same size, and both play an important role in our magickal tides and patterns. Many ancient people described them as the eyes of an important god. Most notably, the Sun is said to be the right eye of the Egyptian God Horus, while the Moon is his left eye, associating the right with solar or direct powers, and the left with lunar or intuitive powers.

The Moon

In planetary magick, every planet is said to "rule" or influence a particular facet of life. The Moon rules magick in general, along with emotional memory, reincarnation, motherhood, children, home, mysteries, and emotional balance. Because it rules magick in general, and Witchcraft in particular, we seek to align with the tides of the Moon to aid our magick.

Generally, when the Moon is waxing, or growing in light, it is the time to do spells to gain things, to manifest tangible results in your life. The closer to the Full Moon you are, the more intense or quick your manifestation can be.

When the Moon is waning, or growing in darkness, it is a time to send things away. Banishments, witherings and diminishments are best. The closer to the dark of the Moon, just before it goes new, the more powerful your magick to decrease and remove influences in your life.

The Moon's phases are divided into quarters astrologically. The first and second quarters are waxing and the third and fourth quarters are waning. The switching point between the second and third is when the Moon goes full, so if you are trying to catch the "tide" of waxing energy, you are best to start your spell or ritual just before the phase turns from second to third quarter.

The change from fourth to first quarter is when the Moon goes new. It's the best time for new projects and slow growth or the declaration of new intentions and plans that will bear fruit over time. It's not a great time for immediate manifestations.

Technically, when the Moon is new, it's still dark to the visible eye, so many wait three days to see the tiny crescent of the Moon's light to do their New Moon rituals, feeling the visual, not the mathematical, is more important in magick. Likewise, some don't seem to care when the Moon is full but technically waning. If it looks full, to them the energy is full.

The Moon can be divided into other segments, but this is the most useful and simplest to know and use. A good Moon calendar, Witch's almanac or astrological calendar will give you the information on the Moon phases. Usually the phase will be indicated somewhere with a simple 1st, 2nd, 3rd, or 4th on the calendar day.

The Sun

The Sun likewise waxes and wanes like the Moon. Spell casters use two different cycles with the Sun. The first and most well-known is the yearly cycle of the Sun. The Sun is waxing from Winter Solstice, also known as Yule, to the Summer Solstice, also known as Litha or Midsummer. The Sun is then waning from the Summer Solstice back to the Winter Solstice. You can use the equinoxes to divide it into quarters, and the Celtic fire festivals of the neopagan Wheel of the Year to divide the cycle into eighths. Magick for increase of light, life force, or gain is best in the waxing part of the year, and magick to go into the dark or diminish is best in the waning time of year, though the harvest technically occurs in the waning year, and most people intuitively feel abundance and blessing at that time of the year.

The least used magickal cycle, but very obvious one, is the daily cycle of the Sun. Popularized by author Dorothy Morrison in her book *Everyday Sun Magic*, the daily cycle can be a powerful alternative to the Moon cycle. We perceive the Sun to be waxing from dawn to noon, and waning from noon to sunset. When the Moon is not in your favor, you can use the daily cycle of Sun, as you only have to wait less than twenty-four hours, not a month.

Beyond the Sun and the Moon, we could go into the detailed art and science of the Zodiac signs, as the Sun, Moon and each planet is said to occupy a sign. The more complex understanding of astrological magick and the placement of the Sun, Moon and other planets in a sign will be detailed in a subsequent volume of this series.

Exercise: When Do You Feel Powerful?

Ask yourself this question, "When do I feel powerful?" Is there a time of day that is better for you? Is there a time that is particularly difficult for you? Does any one season energize you or debilitate you? Do the cycles of the Moon play a part in your empowerment? Do you have a lot of energy and intensity when the Moon is full, or do you feel spacey and ungrounded? Do you feel anything when the Moon is dark or going new? Observe your cycles in relationship to the tides of magickal powers.

One of the first questions asked by new students in magick is, "Do I have to do a spell that fits these cycles perfectly?" Particularly when you are looking at more complex timing involving astrological signs and planetary hours, along with the waxing and waning of the Moon and Sun, it gets harder to plan for the perfect moment. Sometimes in the planning, we can feel so intellectual we are divorced from the flow of life force that is the heart's blood of magick.

The short answer is, "No, you don't." These things are traditional and have survived because people have found value in them. Understanding the patterns and flow of magick is a powerful thing, and intellectual knowledge that helps you feel the flow is the best use of these teachings. But I believe if you feel strongly in your heart that now is the time to do a spell, then do it. Personally I've found the hints, tips and teachings from astrology to be helpful, but I have a love for astrology and not all Witches and magicians do.

Particularly poignant on the topic is a quote from a deceased, well respected and wise Witchcraft elder, Lady Circe, as recorded by her student and initiate, Lady Bona Dea (Patricia DeSandro):

"Witch power is NOW power. The Witches do not wait until the moon is in the correct sign. They are in the NOW and in their mind the moon is always in the correct sign."

Use astrological timing to help you when it helps, but remember the power of magick is in the now, even if you don't self-identify as a Witch. Toltec "witch" Florida Donner says in her book, *The Witch's Dream*, "All of us have a bit of witch in us."

CHAPTER SEVEN:
WRITING PETITION
SPELLS

Petition spells are one of the simplest and most effective forms of magick I've ever encountered. They are particularly great for beginners as they not only use your own magickal skills, but make a direct petition to the divine powers to help align and fuel the magick. They often flow easily and require little in terms of magickal tools and exotic accoutrements.

As I have said, my first petition spell, during a Full Moon magick circle, was for healing a friend of mine and her unborn baby. Both were in grave danger due to malnutrition and a difficult pregnancy. Doctors did not expect both to live. In my petition, I asked for not only the health and safety of the young mother and child, but for the labor to be as "easy as possible." Six weeks later she gave birth, with a labor of only two hours. In the interim of the spell to birth, she gained weight and nutrition, showed stable life signs, and the baby shifted in the womb, all making the birth quite literally as easy as possible. She was up and walking around a few hours later, wondering what the fuss was about its being life threatening. Both mother and child are doing fine to this day.

While I admit her good Italian Catholic family was praying furiously for her, doing novenas, rosaries, and lighting candles in Church, all forms of magick in my eyes, the result was beyond miraculous to me. Thankfully, I kept good magickal records in my journal upon the urging of my first teacher, and could go back and read, "easy as possible," in my spell notes, or I would not have believed it.

To me, this indicated something was working with this whole spell casting and Witchcraft scenario, and I needed to do more research. When subsequent spells also came true, and I got verifiable results and a success rate that was far better than coincidence, I was hooked into studying more deeply and going into meditation and psychic development as well.

The important thing to realize in this process was that I was not a believer. I had no training. I didn't have any magickal charge built up in me through practice or any specific powers of concentration or discipline. I was an open skeptic, ready to experience and determine what made sense to me but equally open to the possibility this was all nonsense and I could put it to rest if it didn't work.

But I did follow the technique. I did follow the "prescription" listed as the method of casting a spell and holding ritual. I followed the recipe and I had success. There are reasons for tradition in spell casting. It's not dogma. It's effectiveness. The procedures should not be disregarded without knowing what they do and if they need to be replaced with something else.

Huna author Serge Kahili King states, in his book *Urban Shaman,* that "effectiveness is the measure of truth." If something works for you, then it is true for you. Things that are passed on have been proven to be true for many different people, hence their effectiveness. Once you understand how things work and have some success, you can experiment in changing techniques and, through intuition and trial and error, pioneer new ways that might be true for other people as well, adding to the body of magickal lore.

Spells as Prayers

Although spells are described to the non-magickal as a form of prayer, this is only half true. Prayers are done in supplication, often with a sense of unworthiness. Some pray as if they are begging. When you enter into a relationship feeling unworthy and having to beg, your spell is generated with that energy. People who do such prayer often bargain with the divine. I'll give up something if you give me this. Or I'll take on something harmful if you take it away from a loved one. How often has a parent asked to take on a child's illness instead of simply praying for the cure alone?

Such a relationship is not in the spirit of modern magick, which is cooperative and co-creative, and even a look into history will show many spells have much more of a sense of authority and command, a definitive sense of worthiness and right, rather than begging. Ancient spells sometimes err too much on the other side, diminishing the role of the spirits or divinities and commanding them without due honor or consent. Many medieval grimoires threaten the powers that are summoned with punishment, which is equally unbalanced.

We would do well to look at many indigenous and native traditions that call to the spirits, rather than command or beg, and simply ask in deep connection and divine communion as a child of the Earth and Universe. Polite and respectful communion is simply the method of best exchange with the divinities and powers of nature. We are all one on some level, so we are simply asking our family for aid, and offering our aid in reciprocal balance.

Yet, petitions are the most akin to prayers as many people know prayer, as they are a direct communion with and request for something from the divine, however you see the divine. The difference is there is an automatic assumption of the truth of the statement, that it is already done on another level, and the spell simply accesses that magick level. While a petition might be phrased as a "want," it usually ends with an affirmation that says in some manner, "It is so," making a seeming request into a cooperative declaration.

Many traditional practitioners, looking to folk magick, say that petition spells such as the ones outlined in this chapter are modern and new, with no history as a true magickal practice. Yet it was the first type of magick I learned from a Witch claiming descent from a traditional folk magick group traced back to Kent, England, predating the modern revival of Wicca.

If you look to the lore of curse tablets, believe it or not, from ancient Greece to Roman occupied Britain, you'll find a technique very similar to petitions. Perhaps some are mislabeled curses, as most typically these petitions carved into lead were for justice and retribution for a wrong, often involving stolen goods. They would be addressed to chthonic powers of the underworld, deities believed to mete out justice and vengeance for wrongs, and a petition stating the crime and the suspected perpetrator would be made, with a request for return of the stolen goods and justice against the wrongdoer. While a bit more wrathful than our modern day petition spells, you'll find the format and technique quite similar, indicating a historic context revived in our modern occult movement.

Likewise, you'll find a lot of written spells from the Egyptian tradition. Possibly no other culture fascinates the occultist more than Egyptian, with its hieroglyphic writing. Spells would be written on papyrus paper, painted on pottery, or carved upon temples and tombs. To commit something to word, either spoken, or particularly written, was to commit its reality to the universe. *The Coffin Texts*, or the later *Book of Coming Forth by Day* (popularly known as *The Egyptian Book of the Dead*) is not only a guide book to the afterlife, but also a series of spells and magick words to aid the deceased on the journey of the afterlife.

Composing Effective Petition Spells

Petition spells can be as easy as simply asking for what you want to manifest or banish in your life. They can be direct and heartfelt. They can be intense and personal. They can be nonchalant and read like a laundry list. They can be angry. They can be filled with joy. Ideally, having a clear intention, strength of will, and method to direct energy will bring some form of power to the spell, be it in emotional strength, sharp and direct clarity, or spiritual connection.

Following in established traditions, I've found the most effective petition spells have five parts to them. They are:

Announcement
Evocation
Intent
Conditions
Gratitude

Announcement – An announcement states who you are. It establishes your identity to the powers you are petitioning. Doesn't the universe know you already? Don't the gods have an inkling of who you are? Yes, of course, but by stating your name, you are gathering your personal will and saying, "I want this." It's not to happen to someone else, somewhere else, but for me, here and now, under the conditions I state. For many, the use of a magickal name is effective. It establishes a magickal persona that is empowered to do the magick. Many take magickal names when they join traditions, dedicate, or initiate upon a specific path. The name establishes them in the magickal current of the tradition. But you don't need a magickal name to effectively cast a spell. Your legal birth name will do just fine.

Evocation – Evocation means the calling of spirits, powers, and divinities to appear. Usually it refers to a visible or tangible appearance: either some sign is given in nature, or the spirit manifests in smoke, candle flame, or to the inner psychic vision. It is technically different from invocation, which usually means summoning the spirits into your body, although in literature, invocation and evocation are used interchangeably and without a distinction to simply mean calling the spirits or power. By evoking the power you wish to communicate, you are establishing a link. Are not the gods/powers/universe ever present? Yes, but by declaring yourself in the announcement, and declaring the power you wish to work with, you are opening a clear line of communication for an effective spell. You don't want to ask the universe for something when the universe isn't really listening to you. Ritual, spells and the structure of these petition spells are the ways to get an open line to the universal powers and have successful results to your magick.

Intent – The intention is the meat of the petition. It is a request or declaration of what you want to manifest. State your intention in as clear and precise terms as possible. It is said by magickal practitioners that the magick always takes the road of least resistance. So while your intention is most important, make sure you say what you mean and mean what you say. If there is a way your spell can correctly manifest by virtue of what you said, but not necessarily what you intended, and that manifestation requires less energy and effort, then the magick will often manifest to fulfill the letter of your intention. When formulating your intention, think about how your life will be different when the intention comes true. Use all your inner senses to envision your new life. Feel it. See it. Hear it. Smell it. Taste it. Try to capture that clarity in words. Be as concise and direct as possible without any ambiguity.

Conditions – Conditions are the stipulations you desire around your manifestations. You don't necessarily want your desired outcome at all costs, do you? If you ask for a million dollars and get hit by a truck and get a million dollar settlement, would that satisfy you when you can't walk or talk? Probably not. So you need to stipulate what you want in such a way that is satisfying to you without closing too many doors of possibility. You don't want to specify the exact way your intention comes to you, as the universe is full of possibilities, and if you close the doors to much of the possible, you lower your chance of success. Always use the intention for what your ultimate goal is, not the means of achieving it. Many people cast money spells, but they usually want the money for something. If you want a vacation, don't ask for the money for the vacation. Ask for the vacation itself. Focus on the details that are important to you, such as location or length of time, and less on the other details. If you really want a car and you want it to be red, make sure you put red in the spell. If the color doesn't matter at all to you, leave it open to create more possible avenues of manifestations where the spell can come true. Good stipulations include:

- ✦ For the highest good, harming none.
- ✦ For the good of all involved.
- ✦ For my highest good.
- ✦ In accord with Divine Will (Or True Will).
- ✦ In accord with the Seed Blueprint for Life.
- ✦ By Divine Providence.
- ✦ Completely acceptable to me on all levels.
- ✦ Completely satisfactory to me in all ways.

A favorite from Witchcraft author and pioneer in the Craft, Sybil Leek, is to write on the back, "In no way will this spell reverse, or place upon me any curse." I have a friend who ends all her spells with, "I ask for this or something better for my highest good." None of her spells work, showing a certain disconnect between her true purpose and her conscious mind, but she always gets something great within the month.

Also remember that what you want now is not necessarily what you want in the future, so a condition can be what is known as a "time lock," which forces the spell to manifest in a specific time frame or expire. I ask for things within six months or within a year, and if it doesn't manifest, I can reevaluate. Many traditions say that spells will always manifest in a lunar cycle if they work, but I haven't found that to be the case. I've done some long term spells at the New Moon that bore fruit many months later. I have a teacher whose request for a very specific kind of table manifested many years after she cast the spell. She thought it had failed, and while she enjoys the table, it's not always helpful for a spell to take years to manifest. I was taught that "as soon as possible" is not a good condition, as the current established conditions might make "as soon as possible" your next lifetime. But "immediately" indicates now, and can change the conditions to make it happen immediately.

Gratitude – Gratitude is a posture of thanks for the spell, with the attitude that it has already happened, turning the spell from a request to a fact. This affirmation at the end can be considered the secret sixth step to the petition. Thankfulness also closes out the relationship with the power or divinity we have called.

Thankfulness puts us into a mindset focusing on what blessings we have, and manifesting more blessings as your attention is placed in that direction. If you want to change your apparent "luck," start a gratitude journal and write down five things you are thankful for each day. See how things change for you.

The format of a standard petition in the Witchcraft traditions I learned and teach would be:

I, (state your name or magickal name), ask in the name of the Two Who Move As One in the love of the Great Spirit, the Goddess and the God, to grant me/remove from me (state your intent). I thank the Goddess and the God for all favors and ask this be in a spirit that is correct and for the good of all involved, harming none. So mote it be.

For those looking for the five parts, they are:

+ **Announcement:** I (state your name or magickal name),
+ **Evocation:** ask in the name of the Two Who Move As One in the love of the Great Spirit, the Goddess and the God,
+ **Intention:** to grant me/remove from me (state your intent).
+ **Gratitude:** I thank the Goddess and the God for all favors
+ **Conditions:** and ask this be in a spirit that is correct and for the good of all involved, harming none.
+ **Declaration:** So mote it be.

The declaration of modern Witches and Wiccans, as well as Freemasons, is "So mote it be," an archaic way of saying "It is so," "So it is/will be" or "So may it be." A Christian or Jewish magician might say "Amen," meaning "I believe" or "So be it." Egyptian style magicians might use the Sun god name Amun, which some think is the source of the word Amen, as the creative force. The term kia can be used as a declarative by followers of the ground-breaking magician Austin Spare, who referred to it as a state of "in-betweenness" or "neither-neither" that is the source of magick, a cosmic desire that some might see as part of the Higher Self or akin to what Crowley called the True Will. "So be it." "It is so" and "It is done" are also used by some who shy away from specific religious terminology.

Writing Out Spells

While petitions can simply be spoken, they tend to be most effective when written down. Just like a motivational speaker telling you to write your goals out and look at them in black and white, writing out and looking at your spell can give it a manifestation, an anchor or gravity in the real world that echoes the tangible results it will soon manifest for you.

Write your spell, ideally by hand, not typed or computer printed, on "virgin parchment." For today's magician, this is a fancy way of saying unused, clean paper. Parchment was often scraped to remove old writing, as we would erase today. Recycled paper can also carry the intentions of the past, so any recycled paper must be cleansed as you'd cleanse yourself or a ritual object – with cleansing incense, oils, or strong energy with intention.

Make the spell as clear, neat and free of mistakes as possible when writing out your ritual copy. I always write a "scrap" copy for my magickal journal later, but make the ritual copy as perfect as possible. If I make a mistake, I start again. If I make three mistakes, then I contemplate the spell. Am I being "saved" by a higher power from doing it? Is there a reason? Or am I self-sabotaging?

You can coordinate the color of paper and/or the color of ink used with your intention:

✦ **Black/White** – All purpose. Most spells are black ink on white paper.

+ **Red** – Power, passion, sex, love, fire, protection, intensity, blessing
+ **Orange** – Communication, information, legal work, writing, creativity, optimism
+ **Yellow/Gold** – Success, wealth, health, happiness
+ **Green** – Love, money, healing, relationships, home
+ **Blue** – Communication, clarity, peace, life force, spirituality
+ **Purple** – Psychic power, past lives, healing, home

Often complementary colors, opposites on the color wheel, and known as "flashing colors" in the traditions of ceremonial magick, are helpful in generating both an altered state and magickal power. After I pick my paper color, I try to use the complementary color of ink. For dark paper colors, it can be hard to use lighter colored inks, such as blue paper with orange ink, unless using an opaque paint, or paint-like pen.

Paper	Ink
Black	White
Red	Green
Orange	Blue
Yellow	Purple
Green	Red
Blue	Orange
Purple	Yellow
White	Black

You can even use magickal inks and a dipped "quill" pen to add power to your spells. You can make these simple ink recipes. While many magickal shops sell inks with such names, if they are commercially prepared, they are most often just colored ink with a magickal label. I suggest making your own by adding a pinch of these herbs and resins, or by adding a drop or two of their essential oil to your own ink bottle, or only use prepared inks by a magician you know and trust. More complex ink recipes include chips of stones, to add the vibration of the mineral to the ink's power. Other ink recipes will be included in a future volume on potions.

Basic Magickal Ink
- All Purpose -
Black Ink
Frankincense Resin
Myrrh Resin
Dragon's Blood Resin

Dragon's Blood Ink
- For Protection, Power and Luck Magick -
Clear Alcohol
Gum Arabic
Red Ink or Food Dye
Dragon's Blood Resin

Dove's Blood Ink
- For Love Magick -
Red (or Purple) Food Dye or Ink
Clear Alcohol
Gum Arabic
Dragon's Blood Resin
Rose or Rose Geranium Essential Oil

Bat's Blood Ink
- For Binding, Hexing and Curses and Breaking Them -
Red or Blue Food Dye or Ink

Clear Alcohol
Gum Arabic
Indigo
Myrrh Resin
Ground Cloves
Cinnamon Oil

Butterfly Blood Ink
- For Communication, Clarity and Blessing -
Yellow Food Dye or Ink
Clear Alcohol
Saffron
Gum Arabic

Raven's Blood Ink
- For Magick Power, Knowledge, Divination, Help in Seemingly Helpless Situations -
Red or Black Food Dye or Ink
Gum Arabic
Clear Alcohol
Iron Oxide Powder

Forest Ink
- For Healing, Growth, Nature, and Prosperity -
Green Ink or Food Dye
Clear Alcohol
Pine Resin
Oakmoss Herb or Essential Oil
Patchouli Herb or Essential Oil

Oak Gall Ink (Iron Gall Ink)
- All Purpose Natural Ink -
Iron Nails

Jar
Distilled Vinegar
Oak Gall, Crushed

Iron Gall or Oak Gall Ink is a historic ink that uses a mixture of iron and plant tannins. Here is a simple recipe you can make easily at home. Start with a few iron nails and distilled vinegar in a jar, letting the acidic vinegar dissolve the iron from the nails. Gather oak galls, the "balls" formed on oak trees from the interaction with the oak and usually an insect or infection. Crush them and pour boiling water upon the crushed gall in a Pyrex dish. Mix the two liquids together to form an ink that will darken over time, though many feel it loses its usefulness so it should be made fresh. Oak gall combines the magick of oak, a Jupiterian tree of leadership, strength and good fortune, with iron, a metal of protection and power.

Walnut Ink
- All Purpose Natural Ink -
Black Walnuts
Alcohol
Gum Arabic

To make this ink, the black walnuts must be gathered in the fall, especially the black, rotting walnuts. The rind of the walnut is the key ingredient, but gather them all up, being warned they will stain your hands and clothing. Put them in a plastic bag and let them all rot, particularly if they are still green. They will get mold and often have insect larvae in them. Once they are black, break them up into smaller pieces. You can smash or hammer them. Then place the walnuts in a stainless steel pot you don't plan on using for household cooking. Cover with water and let them soak for at least a day, longer if possible. When ready, put them on a medium-low heat, simmering them for many hours. Test the liquid with a brush upon paper, to see how dark the liquid's stain is. When it's dark enough to write with, the ink is almost done, and the water has probably cooked down a lot at this point. Let the liquid cool and strain it, separating the walnut pieces from the liquid. A pair of nylons can work well, as well as cheesecloth or a coffee filter. The liquid is now your ink, but it should be preserved. Some use distilled vinegar or sea salt, which is fine for magickal spells you'll be burning. Denatured alcohol is the best preservative, making it about 10-20% by volume of the whole ink. Gum arabic can be added to thicken it.

Use the gum arabic to thicken the inks to your desired consistency. Shake them up before use, to mix the herbs and oils together, as these recipes will naturally have some settling at the bottom of the bottle. Many will also add chips of stones and crystals to the ink, though it's less traditional. Clear quartz adds power to all of the inks, though you can also match the color of the stone, or its associated names and chemical colors, to the color of the ink. Red inks work well with small garnets, red jasper, bloodstone, and also hematite, as the shiny silver stone is actually iron oxide. Jet and obsidian work well in the black ink. Amethyst is good for purple ink, citrine for yellow ink, aventurine for green ink, and blue lapis lazuli for blue ink.

In your ritual, recite your spell. You can do so only once, or if you like, three times, for the three levels of being: conscious mind, subconscious mind, and the super conscious mind. Then dispose of the spell paper, raising the cone of power to release the energy, particularly if you are performing a magick circle ritual for your spells. Spells can be disposed of with the four elements:

- ✦ **Fire** – Burn the spell in a cauldron, thurible (incense burner) or other flameproof container. The ashes can be saved in an ash pot, or disposed of, as with the other elements.
- ✦ **Air** – Rip up the spell and scatter the pieces to the wind.
- ✦ **Water** – Dispose of the spell in water. Use running water to manifest something and stagnant water to banish something.
- ✦ **Earth** – Bury the spell paper so it will return to the earth. Some feel that this method is best for getting rid of things. As the paper rots, so, too, does whatever you wish to banish, metaphorically rotting from your life.

Some will just carry the spell with them in a colored cloth bag matching their intention, or leave it on the altar or another sacred spot in the home until it manifests, and then dispose of it. When saved in such a manner, the paper is often folded towards the user when doing a waxing Moon manifestation spell, or away from the user if doing a banishment waning Moon spell. The number of folds towards or away can have magickal signifigance too. Most common are multiples of three or four. If the spell is written on a long strip of biodegradable paper or cloth, it can be tied to a tree or bush to be released to nature.

Magickal Scripts

While there are many ancient magickal languages, complete with their own structure, grammar and syntax, there are a number of scripts that are used in substitution for Latin alphabet letters. The use of these scripts in spell writing can add a mystique and charm to the magick, and some believe there is inherent power in the characters themselves.

The most popular of these scripts is known as the Theban Script, attributed to Honorius of Thebes. It is also known as the Witch's Alphabet, popularized by Cornelius Agrippa in his *Three Books of Occult Philosophy*, but it was his teacher Johannes Trithemius who first published it. Strangely, it is not used in any of the grimoires attributed to Honorius. It corresponds to the Latin alphabet, though the modern letters of J, U and W are not part of it. I is used for J, V is used for U, and two V's, or VV, are used for W.

Gerald Gardner, founder of modern day Wicca, made a bracelet using Theban characters, and used it to test an "occultist" who said he was a reincarnation of Agrippa. When the occultist didn't recognize the script and claimed it was an ancient Celtic relic, Gardner exposed him. Since then, the script has been used in Gardnerian Books of Shadows and many High Priestesses and Priests use a bracelet with their magickal name in Theban. Angelic magicians, such as David Goddard, author of the *Sacred Magic of the Angels*, claim the script represents a lunar angelic language.

A	B	C	D	E	F	G	H	I	J	K	L	M
⟨⟩	⟨⟩	⟨⟩	⟨⟩	⟨⟩	⟨⟩	⟨⟩	⟨⟩	⟨⟩	⟨⟩	⟨⟩	⟨⟩	⟨⟩

N	O	P	Q	R	S	T	U	V	W	X	Y	Z
⟨⟩	⟨⟩	⟨⟩	⟨⟩	⟨⟩	⟨⟩	⟨⟩	⟨⟩	⟨⟩	⟨⟩	⟨⟩	⟨⟩	⟨⟩

Theban Script

Other alphabets popularized by Agrippa in his three books include Celestial, Malachim, and Passing of the River. These are all associated with Hebrew characters, rather than Latin, but many use their English/Latin equivalents, creating a cipher for English, like Theban. Some say it's not a letter for letter substitution, but a phonetic substitution. Passing of the River Script is specifically used phonetically.

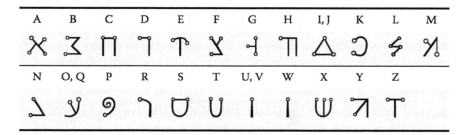

Celestial Script

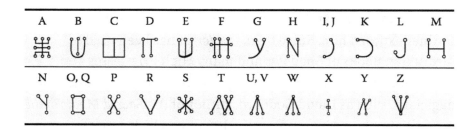

Malachim Script

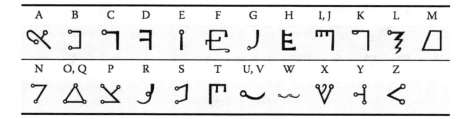

Passing of the River Script

The Casting of Spells

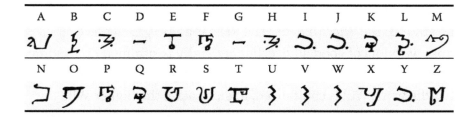

A	B	C	D	E	F	G	H	I	J	K	L	M

N	O	P	Q	R	S	T	U	V	W	X	Y	Z

Alphabet of the Magi Script

Try translating a petition spell into a script to use in your magick.

Ethics and Morals in Spell Casting

While this is a book on spells, not on religion, it is difficult to instruct students in spell casting without getting into morals and ethics. If magick can potentially do anything, one must ask the question, "Just because I can do something, should I do it?" And everyone must answer for themselves.

Much of the theory and personal philosophy discussed here has been about using magick to attune to a higher state of consciousness, a Higher Will, while still manifesting the life you need and want by looking at desire as sacred. But in reality, magick does not have to be practiced that way. It is simply a perspective, a paradigm, that can guide you to a more harmonious way of doing things. But many practitioners discover they do magick with no higher purpose, and if they follow the general guidelines, they can still be successful.

For some, this creates a tremendous weight of responsibility, and many then do not practice magick because of it. For others, it creates a tremendous freedom, so much so, they feel free from the normal restrictions of society baseline ethics, morals, and even laws.

When teaching in a Wiccan magickal context, we are guided by the ethos of the Wiccan Rede. The Rede is a fairly long piece of prose with lots of good advice, but generally is summed up in some form as, "An' it harm none, do as ye Will." My teachers taught me that the word Will is capitalized, to emphasize the higher Will, but most Wiccans learn it with a lower case w. Even so, it emphasizes doing as you desire, as you feel called and seeking to harm none. Contemplate your actions, and if they cause more harm than good, take another approach. Many use it not as a rede, which is good advice, but as a rule, ironclad and immutable. Sadly, because of this, some think it's a law of magick, not an ethical choice, and erroneously believe that magick cannot be used to harm anyone and that some cosmic force, law, or spirit prevents it from happening. A look at any history book on magick will disprove that quite easily. It's as naïve as thinking that guns can only shoot "bad" people and would never be able to harm a "good" person.

As we go deeper into our teachings, one soon realizes that to "harm none" is a virtual impossibility. To eat, we must consume life. Even eating no meat but only vegetables can harm the natural life cycle of the plant. To walk across a field is to step on something alive. To heal an illness is to harm the bacteria or virus that is simply looking to survive and thrive in accord with its nature and own will. So the general advice is really to do as little harm as possible and as much good as possible, in accord with your will and desires.

Traditions outside of Wicca often have less clear ethics and morals. Wicca also believes in the principle known as the Law of Three. Usually it is described as what you do comes back to you threefold, and it is a mechanism as to how magick works. Something as insubstantial as lighting a candle with intention can return to you as a wish manifested because it returned magnified threefold. That magnified energy precipitates down through the astral to form your reality. Old occultists said the universe was built upon a curve, and everything returns to its source, including the physical universe itself. This accounts for our impulse to want to "return" to divinity or "go home."

The Law of Three has undergone a lot of criticism in recent years, as some favor the interpretation that everything occurs on three levels: physical, mental, and spiritual. Some would give it a shamanic spin and say everything occurs on the Middle World, Lower World, and Upper World.

In the ethics of non-Wiccan Witchcraft traditions, the teaching is that one must be able to "pay the coin" of the action, meaning, take responsibility for the consequences of the work, known and unknown. Others simply consider it "paying the price." Many folk magick traditions have nebulous lines between what is considered revenge and cursing and what is considered justice. I myself have no problem with "cursing" a murderer or rapist to be caught or a liar to be exposed. I'm not cursing them to be hit by a train or die of cancer, but intend for the natural mechanisms of justice in our society to get their chance to protect my community.

Practitioners argue that whatever you do, you spiritually open yourself to experiences under similar circumstances. Feri elder Victor Anderson said you must be "free of the sin" that you wish to punish someone for committing. Otherwise, you open yourself up to the same fate. So such magick should not be done lightly or without thought to the consequence. Just because you feel you are free does not mean you haven't committed the same action in another sphere of your life.

In general, I would suggest that you only do magick for things you would take responsibility for in real life. If you wouldn't make it happen through mundane channels, don't make it occur through magickal channels. Some delusional magicians will speak of death magick to their enemies. If it would be illegal for you to kill someone (i.e. anything other than non-premeditated self-defense), then it is spiritually "illegal" to do so through magick. Just because it's magick and the courts of law would not consider it "real" does not mean it isn't. I believe one of the reasons that many magickal practitioners were persecuted in ages past was due to this sense of retribution, making magick illegal. Magick was the resort of the oppressed, but today we all have a more serious chance with normal legal channels when such issues arise.

Most practitioners are not looking at such serious moral issues, but more gray areas, such as love spells, money spells, and healing spells. I aim for win-win situations in all cases, and I do not cast a spell on a specific person without their permission, as I wouldn't want a spell cast upon me without my permission. Spells to attract the "right person" unspecified for love, sex, or friendship are fine with me.

With prosperity and money spells, I never seek to take money away from another, but to fulfill my goal in a way that is for the "highest good." I do not specify anyone else unless they are involved in the job or project and will also benefit mutually from my goal.

In healing spells where I cannot get direct permission, I ask permission of the higher self, with the intention of "if it's not accepted, may the energy be directed to someone/somewhere who does accept it for the highest good."

For more specifically on the ethics and philosophy of money, love and healing, I recommend my previous books, *The Witch's Coin*, *The Witch's Heart*, and *The Inner Temple of Witchcraft*.

The Casting of Spells

"Spell-Checking" Before You Cast

One of the great things about doing group magick is the checks and balances a magickal group can give when learning spell casting. Most covens require members to recite their spell before casting it, so everyone knows to what they are contributing their energy and magick, and there are no surprises once in a ritual circle.

Going around the group reciting spells and getting feedback is an excellent way to find the loopholes in your spells and get some practice in becoming clearer in your intention. If your coven or lodge-mate can misunderstand you, believe me that the universe can also misunderstand. You might think it can't, that it should know your heart and your pure intentions beyond language, but magick is communication and if you are not clear, your result will not be clear.

Here are a few examples:

I, Mary Jo, ask in the name of the Goddess, God, and Great Spirit, to create a perfect life for me that is completely to my satisfaction, for my highest good. I thank you for this perfect life. So mote it be.

While not technically incorrect, a "perfect life" is a little vague. How do you define perfect? What specifically would need to change? Why do you think of your life as imperfect right now? With a spell such as this, so much might need to change that there would not be enough energy. It would be more effective to pick one aspect, change it, and then move onto another, changing your life in increments rather than expecting one spell to fix everything.

I, Michael Smith, ask in the name of the Universe, to be granted an opportunity for career advancement in my chosen field. I thank the power of the Universe and ask this be in accord with divine will, harming none. Amen.

This one is pretty simple. An opportunity is not a new job or promotion or a raise. What do you really want? Focus on that. You might think the opportunity that is in accord with divine will should be perfect, but it could be the perfect opportunity but not the perfect end result. You might interview for a great job, or be considered for a promotion, but never get it. You got the opportunity, not the result. Getting an opportunity doesn't harm you or anyone else. Your disappointment or frustration isn't harm. So it can still manifest, but it is not what you want.

I, Starfinder Pathway, call upon the Divine Mother of the Cosmos to banish all interpersonal conflicts I am having at my job. I ask this be for my highest good and thank you for this blessing. So be it.

With this spell, the result might be the banishment of any opportunities to have conflict by losing the job. And it could be for your highest good, or the good of those involved, to not have you around anymore. But it says nothing about keeping the job if your intention is to keep the job. A better phrase might be "to clear all miscommunications that lead to conflict and prevent me from experiencing a harmonious work environment." It could also benefit from a time frame and perhaps a "totally acceptable to me on all levels" somewhere in there.

Beyond the simple mistakes of spell phrasing, it should go without saying to remember the classic advice – Be careful what you wish for, because you just might get it. Are you sure you really want it? In the wisdom of Oscar Wilde, "When the gods wish to punish us they answer our prayers." I'm not sure if that is a total truth, but in many situations, being unclear in intent, while also vehemently passionate or righteous about it, we often get what we want and it feels like a punishment. From a magician's standpoint, you simply got the result of your magick. It is as neutral and amoral as cause and effect.

The Lust for Results

One of the hardest aspects of spell casting involves what is colorfully known as the Lust for Results. At its most basic level, it is the inability to let go of the energy and intention of the spell once it's cast. When continual focus is given to the spell's intention, often coupled with fear, doubt and anxiety, one quickly pulls the energy from the spell as it works, draining it of any power. Spells that require a simple manifestation work best when the intention is let go and can do its work. Some would describe it as moving from the conscious mind to the subconscious, or psychic mind, to quietly do the work without anxiety or doubt.

Others describe the spell like a thoughtform, a packet of energy that must go forth from the spell caster into the universe to gather the necessary energies to create the conditions to manifest the goal. Every time you think of it, you draw a little bit of your life force from it back to you. If you rob it of too much life force, the spell fails. In either scenario, the spell fails because of your obsession with it, your lust for results, and your fear of lack of results. Your fear creates the very thing you wished to avoid.

The mechanisms of good ritual help us let go. Creating sacred space and closing sacred space is a good way to release and break the connection. Disposing of the petition components is another way – burning, ripping or immersing the paper is a visual cue to let it go. Other traditions of magick have other triggers for release, such as letting the candle burn away.

Sadly there is not one tried and true trick for releasing your lust for results. Many believe the more in tune your intention is with your Higher Self, the less anxious you will be about it. Others fear that there is no real way to release it other than time and training. That is why disciplined practice, meditation and mental training go hand in hand with magickal practices for spell casting. By learning to quiet your mind in other situations, you can bring calm to it when you might otherwise have concern. Cleansing and banishing rituals are helpful too. They can clear and banish our obsessive thought patterns and lust for results.

Simply observe what kind of spells have you more anxious than others, how you can channel any of that energy, and when you can release it into absolute certainty for your spell's success rather than fear of failure. Only then can you make this energy work for your success.

Exercise: Write Your Own Spell

Using the examples and teaching above, write your own spell. Once you have done this, review it, and if you feel comfortable with the phrasing and intention, cast your spell. Record your wording and your experience with the spell in a journal or other magickal record and let it go. Look back in the coming months to see if your magick worked.

Psychic Writing

Though not a traditional petition spell or written talisman, there is a method of magick known simply as psychic writing. Popularized in the work of the psychic Jose Silva, creator of the Silva Mind Control Method, one simply uses intention, visualization and will to "write" a word or phrase in the air in a room, upon a wall, on an object, or even more controversially, upon

The Casting of Spells

a person. Usually the writing is imagined in "cursive" script, and you can write it out with your finger as you visualize it, or simply hold it in your mind. For future generations not learning cursive script, I imagine block printing can work just as well, though my first inclination is to do it the way I learned it with cursive.

This technique imprints a specific psychic energy in the atmosphere, which can change the environment and affect the outcome of actions and events. For example, when trying to claim a space as yours for a time, you can psychically write your name upon all four walls, ceiling and floor, marking your territory. It's a powerful technique to use when you are coming into a new room, such as a classroom when you are the teacher, to set the right tone that you are in charge. If you're not in charge, but you want to change the environment of a chaotic room, write the word peace on all the walls before things start. Notice how the room changes.

I've learned that, like affirmations, it's best to stick with "positive" statements. Using the word safe is better than no accident, as many believe our consciousness will only hear the word accident when using simple statements like this in magick.

You are only limited by your imagination. Here are some ideas:

"Safe" written on your vehicle or home
"Health" written on your body
"Wealth" upon your wallet or checkbook
"Grow" upon your plants and trees
"Invisible" on yourself when you don't want to be seen
"Look at me" when wanting attention or presenting to a group
"Leave" in the room when someone won't leave you alone

Explore the uses of psychic writing and see what you can come up with to fulfill your own needs and desires.

Chapter Eight: Incantations

Incantations are spoken or chanted spells that are not necessarily written down and released in a formal ritual. While they can be done in a magick circle, more often than not they are done as needed in daily life. They are an effective form of magick to use when you don't have ritual tools or the time and space to do a full ritual.

Incantations are the classical form of magick words that everyone seeks out, not realizing the power is not necessarily in the words themselves, but in both the spell caster and their repeated successful use. Incantations can be made by the user for specific instances, but some are handed down through folklore and build up a charge, a bank or battery of energy from the successes. Often someone with little magickal knowledge can still use them successfully due to that charge.

Some incantations involve special words that are from foreign languages or made-up words that have no etymology at all. The classic example is Abracadabra, which was originally a written charm with diminishing characteristics, used to diminish illness when worn close to the chest and then disposed of in water.

There are a lot of popular meanings assigned by magicians to the word itself, with the most popular being, "I create as a I speak." This isn't universally accepted, with other possible translations being, "I create like the word," "It came to pass as it was spoken," and an abbreviation for the Hebrew words of Father, Son and Holy Spirit, the Gnostic god Abraxas, or even a mnemonic device for the start of the alphabet, ABCD.

```
ABRACADABRA
ABRACADABR
ABRACADAB
ABRACADA
ABRACAD
ABRACA
ABRAC
ABRA
ABR
AB
A
```

Abracadabra

Many practitioners of these sacred tongues believe the tone and vibration of the sound has inherent power. Each has a vibration and an archetypal force. These words are embodiments of power. They can be used alone or added to incantations in your own language. Sacred words have become part and parcel of the ceremonial magician's art, invoking energies through the use of Hebrew, just as the yogi would use Sanskrit. Folk magick practices are filled with words that are now barbarous names, misspelled and corrupted, of spirits and deities that are no longer recognized, yet they have power.

Another theory on these words is that nerves and energies are stimulated when speaking them correctly, with the lips and tongue striking acupressure points on the roof of the mouth in specific patterns. The shift of the spell caster's personal energy is what fuels the intention, not any inherent power in the sound.

Perhaps all of these theories hold some truth, but I think incantations are ultimately ways of focusing intention, just as a petition or a candle does. And when studying foreign sounds, it is important to remember your native tongue (and for most of us reading this, it's English) is still very powerful in making magick. Because you understand it clearly, it can be your best vehicle for spoken spells to work successfully.

Incantations as Ritual

A proper incantation doesn't need a full ritual, as it contains all the elements of a good spell ritual. Even if it's short, the pattern, meter, or in general, the oddness of the incantation is a sufficient shift from our everyday speaking and listening to alter our consciousness. Many incantations are in a very sing-song pattern and rhythm. While they don't always make great poetry, the pattern helps induce trance.

One of the earliest uses of the term charm involves what we now call incantations. Charms were spoken, alone, or over a simple ritual object, a talisman or an amulet, that most of us now refer to as charms like a charm bracelet. The spoken charm could magickally "charm" or induce an altered state in the listener. For some, it could be a form of mesmerism or distraction. Many stage show illusionists use the technique in their stage patter, to distract your attention from what they want to hide, and draw your attention to something unimportant but flashy, allowing them to produce their illusion. We can use the same techniques knowingly to induce a self-trance, just as ritual does.

The word rune can also be used for an incantation. Most assume the meaning of rune today refers to the Norse and Anglo-Saxon magickal symbol systems, the Elder Futhark and Younger Futhark, though in past times, a rune, like a charm, referred to a spoken spell. Most famous is "The Witch's Rune" in the Gardnerian Book of Shadows, attributed to Gerald Gardner and Doreen Valiente.

Incantations use powerful imagery, often visual or emotional, to stimulate the magickal fire to make their events happen. They are almost in the form of short stories with their powerful images. Like a good ritual, they evoke image and emotion to set the magick into effect.

They can be effective for people who do not do well visualizing. Many of us have trouble when told to close our eyes, focus, and make something appear in our mind's eye. While it's the favored form of modern magick and self-help, it can be artificial. But all of us have had the experience of images rising when listening to a story or poem. We don't force it. They just come because of the powerful words. It's easy to see how the ancients, using their spells, were visualizing, yet very little literature emphasizes it as we do today in magick. That's probably because stories were such an integral part of life, religion, and most importantly, entertainment. No televisions, movies, and computer screens for the ancients!

And like ritual, incantations have a clear beginning, middle and end to them. When you are done reciting the spell, you are done. It's a clear sign to let go and let it manifest now that your work is done.

Traditional Incantations

Some of the most effective traditional incantations passed down include those from the American tradition of Pennsylvania Dutch Folk Magick, also known as Pow-wow.

To Pull the Heat from Burns

Two angels came down from the north;
one named Fire, the other Frost;
Frost said to Fire go away, go away;
in the name of Jesus go away.

— *Pow-Wows, or Long Lost Friend,* by John George Hoffman

To Stop Bleeding

I walk through a green forest;
There I find three wells, cool and cold;
The first is called courage,
The second is called good,
And the third is called stop the blood.

— *Pow-Wows, or Long Lost Friend,* by John George Hoffman

Another Method of Stopping Fire

Our dear Sarah journeyed through the land,
having a fiery hot brand in her hand.
The fiery brand heats; the fiery brand sweats.
Fiery brand, stop your heat
fiery brand, stop your sweat.

— *Pow-Wows, or Long Lost Friend,* by John George Hoffman

Modern Witches and Wiccans use a variety of incantations, some drawn from traditional sources, others just inspired by them. This "Healing Rune" is used in many Witchcraft traditions, and has elements in common with both European and American folk magick incantations. I first found it in the book *Wicca* by Viviane Crowley.

Wiccan Healing Rune

This is the spell that we intone,
Flesh to flesh and bone to bone.
Sinew to sinew and vein to vein,
And each one shall be whole again.

The Witch's Rune is used to raise power. Also known in some circles as "The Ancient Call."

The Witch's Rune

Darksome night and shining moon,
Hearken to the Witches' rune.
East, then south, west then north,
Here come I to call thee forth.
Earth and water, air and fire,
Work ye unto my desire.
Wand and Pentacle and Sword
Hearken ye unto my word.
Cords and Censer, Scourge and Knife,
Waken all ye into life.
Power of the Witches Blade,
Come ye as the charm is made.
Queen of Heaven, Queen of Hell,
Lend your aid unto the spell.
Horned Hunter of the Night,
Work my will by magic rite.
By all the power of land and sea,
As I do will, so mote it be.
By all the might of moon and sun,
Chant the spell and be it done.

The Casting of Spells

A traditional charm I also learned first from the writings of Doreen Valiente *(Witchcraft for Tomorrow)* is known as the Nine Knot Spell, though there are several variations. It can be used for any intention, but you recite this incantation as you knot a string:

Nine Knot Spell

By the knot of one
The spell's begun.
By the knot of two
It cometh true.
By the knot of three
Thus shall it be.
By the knot of four
'Tis strengthened more.
By the knot of five
So may it thrive.
By the knot of six
The spell we fix.
By the knot of seven
The Stars of Heaven.
By the knot of eight
The hand of fate.
By the knot of nine
The thing is mine.

Usually the knots are tied in this pattern upon the string:

---1---6---4---7---3---8---5---9---2---

Another modern Witch's incantation that has gained popularity is known as the Squat Parking Spot incantation. In truth, it is more of a thoughtform, a semi-independent magickal construct,

...e people who use it. The idea is that there is a "...deva" or "parking spirit/goddess" named Squat, ...ialized as a large black woman in a meter maid ...ooking for a space, you simply put your thumb and ...together, like an "OK" sign and say:

Squat, Squat, find me a spot.

Keep repeating the spell until you find a spot. When you do, thank her, and if there is no meter involved, drop a few pennies on the ground near the spot as an offering.

In working my own incantations, I created this set to empower a series of charms designed as pocket charms manufactured by Deva Designs. They are inscribed on the back of talismans, used to activate and empower the designs, but they work quite well on their own as simple spoken charms.

Ancient Wisdom
With Rays of Light
To the mystic eye
Grant me the secret knowledge
Of the Wise
Let me walk with the ancient ones
With the blessings of the Stars, Moon, and Sun.

Use before rituals and spells to gain a connection to the threads of ancient wisdom that flow from our ancestors. This helps empower us before any magickal working.

Career Success
With fire, water, earth and air

By the four points of the compass square
Power to success in my career.
Complete success fills my sphere.
So mote it be!

Recite not simply for prosperity, but to guide you to the right vocation.

Dreams

By the Moon pools that call me,
May the Dreaming Spirits hear.
Open the gates of Horn,
And grant me dreams true and clear.
Hail and welcome!

Use before bedtime to trigger lucid dreams, spirit contact and magick while you sleep.

Fertility & Creativity

Creation from the Cosmic Womb.
Spinning fate upon the loom.
Power flows to this birth.
Creating something new upon the Earth.
So mote it be!

This charm has been used both for traditional forms of fertility, for those having difficulty conceiving a child, and more creative forms of "birth" such as an artistic or community endeavor.

Grounding

Feet on the Earth
Roots digging down.

Present in body, mind and spirit
Anchored from my soles to my crown.
So mote it be!

Use this after visionary experiences to return yourself back to the here and now, centered in your body, place and time.

Healing
With serpents rising and flower blooms,
For Life's sake from the cosmic womb,
Healing powers flow through me.
Make me hale and whole.
So mote it be!

Evoke healing powers for both physical ailments and other issues of health and well being.

Love
By the Star of the Morning,
And the Star of the Eve,
By the Light of the Lady,
And the Three Who Weave,
I invoke Love into my life,
Romance and Pleasure
I open my heart
To Venus' Treasures.
So mote it be.

Use to both evoke a sense of self-love, and for romance.

Magickal Power
By the Three Rays of Magic,

Within the Witching Hour,
By the Five Stars of the North,
I summon forth true Magick Power.
So mote it be!

Like ancient wisdom, use this to invoke magickal power within yourself prior to a working or ritual.

Prosperity

By the twelve Suns of the Year,
From which all things grow,
Grant me blessings and riches,
With your Golden Glow.
Success and good fortune,
Turn towards me.
Fulfill my ambitions,
And grant me Prosperity.
So mote it be!

Use to gain prosperity and wealth in a manner that supports your overall well-being.

Protection

By the three rings of light,
And five points of power,
By the Horns of the God,
And the Thorns of the Flower,
Protected from all harm am I,
By Blessings Divine.
Protected from injury, illness or malice.
Victory is mine.

ʳotection incantation to help conjure energies that
n.

Psychic Sight
Blessed Moon hanging in the night,
Open the left eye and open the right.
Open all of my senses to see and to know.
Open the psychic eye,
And let my intuition flow.
So mote it be.

Speak this charm before doing psychic work such as tarot or rune readings. Also use it repeatedly if you feel that you need to increase your intuitive abilities overall.

Safe Travel
With the wanderer's blessings,
May the path be illuminated,
By the Sun, Moon and Stars.
May all my journeys be safe,
Near and far.
So mote it be!

A charm to be said before undertaking any major travel.

Spirit Contact & Meditation
Open the Gates. Open the Veil.
Show me the keepers of the mystery grail.
Let me speak to spirit beyond.
Hear me guides,
Hear and respond!
So mote it be.

The Casting of Spells

Use this before meditating to help you commune more deeply with your spiritual allies.

Spiritual Evolution

With the Spiraling Line of Mystery
I seek to evolve my soul
To be clear and free
By those who come before
And come after me
Creating a world of pure harmony.

While not as clear as some more base intentions, the spiritual evolution incantation can be recited to help us understand the ever evolving patterns in our lives and how we can work with them.

Wishes

By the Nine Sisters
Holding the Nine Cups of Blessing
May my dreams come into view
By Star, by Stone, By Crescent Moon
Grant this wish
May my Dream be True!

Formulate your wish clearly in your mind. Then recite this spell.

The designs for the accompanying spell coins will be shared in a future volume in this series, on charms, talismans and amulets, yet the incantations work wonderfully well on their own as well. For those seeking to purchase the coins with incantations, please look for a local retailer that carries Deva Design Products.

Invocations, Evocations and Prayers

Along with incantations in magick, there are invocations, evocations and prayers. Often used synonymously, they are all slightly different in a true magickal sense. While incantations might reference an entity or historic figure in its poetry, the power of an incantation is usually based upon the imagery depicted, the words recited and the energy of the spellcaster. The poetry helps focus our energy and will with the intention. Invocations, evocations and prayers, on the other hand, usually are focused upon specific entities or a generalized sense of divinity.

An invocation usually refers to a rite including both a verbal component and an energetic exchange, where a specific entity is brought either into the body of a practitioner or into the magick circle where they perform the ritual. In most Witchcraft traditions, the term invocation means bodily invocation, as the entity goes "in" the practitioner. In many ceremonial magick traditions, the magician is identified with the magick circle, so anything "in" the circle is an invocation. Invocation manifests in a wide range of experiences, with varying degrees of awareness and control on the part of the practitioner. On a minor level, one can feel "overshadowed" by the entity, subtly guiding, or on a major level, fully possessed. Most practitioners have a blend or mix with the entity somewhere between the two.

For most Witches, invocation is used to "draw down" the Goddess or God into a High Priestess or High Priest, who then in turn will commune directly with the coven. For the ceremonial magician, it is deities of ancient lands or archangelic figures who are brought into the circle. Other practitioners use invocation phenomena, but might not call it such. Those who do mediumship with the ancestors, conscious trance channeling with discarnate entities, and full body trance channeling, are all performing a form of invocation. Likewise spiritual possession, be it by the lwa of the Voodou traditions or the Holy Spirit in a charismatic Christian tradition, is also invocation. A typical aspect of invocation is the invocatory poetry used as a ritual trigger.

This invocation of the Moon Goddess is found in the Drawing Down the Moon rite of Gardnerian Wiccans, from the Gardnerian Book of Shadows. This version has been made public and shows us what a classic invocation of the Goddess can look like.

Drawing Down the Moon

High Priestess stands in front of Altar, assumes Goddess position. Magus, kneeling in front of her, draws pentacle on her body with Phallus-headed Wand, invokes:

"I Invoke and beseech Thee, O mighty Mother of all life and fertility. By seed and root, by stem and bud, by leaf and flower and fruit, by Life and Love, do I invoke Thee to descend into the body of thy servant and High Priestess [name]."

The Moon having been drawn down, Magus and other men give Fivefold Kiss:

(kissing feet) "Blessed be thy feet, that have brought thee in these ways";

(kissing knees) "Blessed be thy knees, that shall kneel at the sacred altar";

(kissing womb) "Blessed be thy womb, without which we would not be";

(kissing breasts) "Blessed be thy breasts, formed in beauty and in strength";

(kissing lips) "Blessed be thy lips, that shall speak the sacred names."

Training in true invocation techniques goes beyond the scope of this work, yet one should understand it when performing incantations and spells, to make sure this line is not crossed without proper training and support.

Evocations are often synonymous with invocation, to the point where people use them interchangeably, but technically an evocation is to call an entity to some form of presence of manifestation. It does not enter "in" the body, so it is not an invocation. Most Witches consider a form of evocation is any call for an entity to be present, be it deity, elemental, angel, ancestor, faery, or power animal. Ceremonial magicians create a special space for evoked spirits, usually a Triangle of Manifestation outside of their magick circle space, or evoke spirits within objects, such as crystals or mirrors. Classically the evocation was only a success if the spirit manifested in some tangible way, such as a face in the incense smoke, a shift in the temperature, a noise in the walls, or a sound or a light of some sort. The classic spirit manifestations in the seances of Spiritualist mediums were expected, including the scent of flowers, ringing of tiny bells, knocking tables, and even the manifestations of "ectoplasm." These days ectoplasmic manifestations seem rare or the work of charlatans. Evocations can be considered to be calls or summons to a spirit. They can also be known as conjuring, or conjuring spirits, but should not be confused with the magickal folk tradition known as Southern Conjure. Conjure, like magick, is one of those words with many meanings.

The simple formula of summoning the "mighty ones" of the four directions from the Gardnerian Book of Shadows has become the basis of many other quarter calls in modern Wicca and Witchcraft. They would usually be done in turn, starting with the East and moving clockwise.

"I summon, stir, and Call thee up, thou Mighty Ones of the East, South, West, and North."

Generally an evoked spirit in magickal practices is given a task. In this case, the mighty ones guard the bounds of the magick circle. Evoked spirits from the grimoire traditions—angels, demons, djinn, and other spirits—are given a job to manifest something for the magician.

Lastly on the list is prayer. Prayers are much like our petition spells, petitions to specific or generalized divinity. Some prayers are done by rote, to establish a divine connection. They are often praising the divinity. Others are informal and in your own words, asking for a specific boon. Prayers that evoke power imagery of divinity to empower the intention are some of the most effective forms of prayer.

Here is an Egyptian Hymn to Amun-Ra.

HAIL to thee, Amun-Ra, Lord of the thrones of the earth,
the oldest existence, ancient of heaven, support of all things;

Chief of the gods, lord of truth; father of the gods, maker of men and
beasts and herbs; maker of all things above and below;

Deliverer of the sufferer and oppressed, judging the poor;

Lord of wisdom, lord of mercy; most loving, opener of every eye, source of
joy, in whose goodness the gods rejoice, thou whose name is hidden.

Thou art the one, maker of all that is, the one; the only one; maker of
gods and men; giving food to all.

Hail to thee, thou one with many heads; sleepless when all others sleep,
adoration to thee.

Hail to thee from all creatures from every land, from the height of
heaven, from the depth of the sea.

The spirits thou hast made extol thee, saying, welcome to thee, father of the fathers of the gods; we worship thy spirit which is in us.

A prayer for healing and support used in the Witchcraft traditions is known as the "Amalthean Horn Prayer." Found in the Gardnerian Book of Shadows and its descendants, it is quite similar to Aleister Crowley's poem "La Fortuna," and some feel it demonstrates a connection proving Crowley was the originator of the Book of Shadows, but he was merely an influence, not the only source.

Amalthean Horn Prayer
Hail, Aradia, from the Amalthean horn
Pour forth thy store of Love. I lowly bend
Before Thee! I invoke thee at the end
When other Gods are fallen and put to scorn.
Thy foot is to my lips! My sighs inborn
Rise, touch, curl about thy heart. Then spend,
Pitiful Love, loveliest Pity, descend
And bring me luck who am lonely and forlorn.

And of course there are all sorts of more "traditional" and standard prayers in mainstream religions. Though not considered magickal by the mainstream, prayers like the Hail Mary and the various Psalms are quite magickal and used in spellcraft. The grimoires known as *The Sixth and Seventh Book of Moses* contain information in using Psalms in magick. One of my own mentor's favorite psalms is Psalm 23. Magickally it is said to grant reliable information through dreams, essentially a spell for lucid dreams for problem solving and advice. Spiritually it is for strength and protection in difficult times.

The Casting of Spells

Psalm 23 (KJV)

The Lord is my shepherd; I shall not want.
He maketh me to lie down in green pastures:
he leadeth me beside the still waters.
He restoreth my soul:
he leadeth me in the paths of righteousness for his name's sake.
Yea, though I walk through the valley of the shadow of death, I will fear
no evil: for thou art with me; thy rod and thy staff they comfort me.
Thou preparest a table before me in the presence of mine enemies: thou
anointest my head with oil; my cup runneth over.
Surely goodness and mercy shall follow me all the days of my life:
and I will dwell in the house of the Lord forever.

The instructions for using Psalm 23 is as follows:

Should you desire to receive reliable instructions in regard to something through a vision or in a dream, then purify yourself by fasting and bathing, pronounce the Psalm with the holy name Jah seven times, and pray at the end of each repetition:

Lord of the World! notwithstanding thy unutterable mighty power, exaltation, and glory, thou wilt still lend a listening ear to the prayer of thy humblest creature, and wilt fulfill his desires. Hear my prayer also, loving Father, and let it be pleasing to thy most holy will to reveal unto me in a dream, whether (here the affair of which a correct knowledge is deserved must be plainly stated) as thou didst often reveal through dreams the fate of our forefathers. Grant me my petition for the sake of thy adorable name, Jah. Amen. Selah!

Arcane Tongues & Barbarous Words

Anything foreign to our ear can hold the power of a magick word, yet some languages and sounds originate in cultures where magick was clearly a greater part of life. We have examples of powerful words to create magickal change from both eastern and western traditions. Two of the most powerful and popular examples in modern magick today would be in the form of Sanskrit mantras and runic galdur.

The word mantra originates from the Sanskrit, a sacred language of India and the Hindu traditions, and refers to a sound or series of sounds to create change. Various sounds are associated with divine powers, and a string of sounds and words together have specific meanings and create specific types of change. They are used in the religious practices of Hindus, Buddhists and Sikhs, and now the term mantra has been applied to repetitive sounds for religious and magickal practices from a variety of sources, not just Sanskrit. Hewbrew divine names can be considered Western mantras, for example.

While many are focused on spiritual evolution and development, Western seekers are often primarily focused on mantras that create a magickal change in their life, such as prosperity, healing or good relationships.

Om Gum Ganapatayei Namaha

This mantra is one for general help from the Hindu god Ganesha, the beloved elephant head god. Ganapathi is another name for Ganesha, as the mantra translates to, "Om and salutations to the remover of obstacles [Ganapathi], for which Gum is the seed."

Ganesha's power is to remove obstacles and make things easier for us.

The Casting of Spells

Om Shrim Maha Lakshmiyei Swaha

A mantra for abundance and success to the Hindu goddess Lakshmi. To recite it for forty days straight will transform your relationship with prosperity. It translates as, "Om and salutations. I invoke the great feminine principle of great abundance."

Om Shri Dhanvantre Namaha

A healing mantra invoking Dhanvantre, the Celestrial Physician. While the mantra might not be an instant cure, its intention is to find the appropriate healing path and aid. The words translate as, "Salutations to the being and power of the Celestial Physician."

Om Bhu, Om Bhuvaha, Om Swaha
Om Maha, Om Janaha, Om Tapaha, Om Satyam Om Tat Savitur
Varenyam
Bhargo Devasya Dhimahi Dhiyo Yonaha Prachodayat

Known as the Gayatri Mantra, this complex phrase is a powerful tool for spiritual evolution and enlightenment. It asks for the celestial powers to imbue our chakras with their light, translating as, "O self-effulgent Light that has given birth to the luminous planes of consciousness, who is worthy of worship and appears through the spiritual lens of the sun, illumine our intellect."

Mantra teachers often instruct students under the age of twenty-eight to use the phrase "Namaha" when called for in a mantra, which means "I bow" or "I acknowledge the name" to release the energy, similar to "So mote it be" or "Amen." Those over the age of twenty-eight, meaning they have completed the astrological transit known as a Saturn return, a phase of karmic learning, should replace "Namaha" with "Swaha" which means "I testify." This phrase aligns more strongly with the energy of the "cosmic" adult and a greater awareness of consciousness. Other teachers believe you should use the mantra as it is given to you by a teacher.

The work of Thomas Ashely Farrand brings a practical and authentic use of mantra to the western world. His book *Healing Mantras* is an excellent resource to better understand the art and science of mantra in daily life and has been a guide in my own practice. The mantras above are from his book, as it presents clear phonetic presentations of the mantra with clear translations. I highly recommend all his work.

While Sanskrit is said to be the mother tongue of the Eastern mysteries, Hebrew is often considered to be the base language of the Western mysteries. It is the foundation of Kabalistic traditions which in turn were the basis of the modern magickal revival of Hermetic Qabalah. Each of the heavenly emanations are associated with an astrological planet, an archetypal force, and a "name" of God in Hebrew. Each letter is said to contain a power of the universe, used in the creation of all things. They can be "mapped out" upon a Cube of Space, a symbol of creation, and upon the Tree of Life, another glyph depicting the entire universe, seen and unseen, in the form of ten emanations known as sephiroth.

Sephiroth	Meaning	Planet	Divine Name	Magick
Malkuth	Kingdom	Earth	Adonai ha-Aretz	Balance, Material Gain, Earth Mysteries
Yesod	Foundation	Moon	Shaddai El Chai	Creativity, Reproduction, Dreams, Psychic Abilities, Magick
Hod	Splendor	Mercury	Elohim Tzabaoth	Memory, Learning, Language
Netzach	Victory	Venus	Yod Heh Vav Heh Tzabaoth	Love, Lust, Sexuality, Nature
Tiphereth	Beauty	Sun	Yod Heh Vav Heh Eloah Va-Da'ath	Harmony, Altruism, Success
Geburah	Power	Mars	Elohim Gibor	Power, War, Overcoming Enemies
Chesed	Mercy	Jupiter	El	Prosperity, Good Fortune, Compassion
Binah	Understanding	Saturn	Yod Heh Vav Heh Elohim	Binding, Protection, Creation, Silence

Sephiroth	Meaning	Planet	Divine Name	Magick
Chokmah	Wisdom	Neptune	Yod Heh Vav Heh	Wisdom, Mystery, Generation
Kether	Crown	Pluto/Uranus	Eheieh	Divinity, Source, Pure Awareness

Even beyond the more esoteric and transcendent traditions of Hebrew mysticism, the medieval grimoires are often borrowing words of power from Hebrew, and in the more practical side of magick, such as those found in the *The Sixth and Seventh Book of Moses*, there are specific instructions on how to use the specific letters and names, along with the better known Psalm magick. Here is a list of the letters with their grimoire associations, different from the classic occult associations with planets, paths and tarot cards.

Aleph	Cures shaking and quivering, helps those who bear burdens of vows
Beth	Improves the memory, opens the heart, increases intelligence
Gimel	Heals eye injury and pain
Daleth	Heals left eye injuries, brings success in lawsuits, helps make fortunate decisions
Heh	Stops one from engaging in vice or "sin"
Vav	Makes a "servant" faithful
Zayin	Heals the spleen, heals melancholy, removes you from misled business adventures

Cheth	Cures pains in the upper body through wine
Teth	Cures kidney and liver illness, removes pain in the hips
Yod	Grants grace and favor from the creator and favor from humans
Kaf	Heals sores on right side of nose, heals incurable sores
Lamed	Grants favorable outcome in legal matters
Mem	Heals limb pain, particularly pain or paralysis in the right arm or hand
Nun	Grants safe and prosperous travel
Samech	Grants favorable response from superiors
Ayin	Like Mem, but heals pain in the left arm or hand
Pe	Like Kaf, but heals sores on left side of nose
Tzaddi	Prevents misrepresentation and injustice
Qoph	Heals dangerous or painful injuries of left leg
Resh	Heals running boils in right ear with the aid of onion water
Shin	Heals severe or burning headaches with the aid of olive oil
Tav	Like Resh, heals boils with onion water, but in left ear

The letters are used in conjunction with specific verses in Psalm 119, the longest of the Psalms, as described in the *Books of Moses*, and this grimoire should be referenced for the traditional magick of this system. For example:

Aleph — *The eight verses of this letter, which all begin with Aleph, should be pronounced over a man whose limbs shake and quiver, and if this be done in a low and even tone of voice, he will be relieved. If anyone has made a vow, which has become burdensome to fulfill, it will be easy for him to keep his promise.*

And

Teth — *The division of the letter Teth, verses 65 to 72, is an easy, quick, and tried remedy to cure the severest case of kidney or liver complaints, or to take away pain in the hips. Pronounce these eight verses properly, specially, and reverently over the sick person and he will convalesce.*

And

Lamed— *If you are summoned to appear personally before the Judge in a lawsuit, pray on the preceding day, just after the evening prayer, the division of the letter Lamed, verses 89 to 96, and you will obtain a favorable hearing, and will be permitted to leave the court justified.*

Galdur is the spoken use of the runic traditions of the Norse and Saxons. Each symbol, or rune, in the tradition is not just a pictorial image, but its nature is threefold. A rune is representative of a symbol, or stave, the shape of the lines used to form it. Each shape contains a teaching. A rune is representative of a song or sound. The name of the rune is a magick word. And lastly, a rune contains a mystery, hidden lore about the nature of the universe and the cosmic powers that are a part of it. One could say the shape and song really point to the true mystery of the rune.

To chant or sing spells in the Northern European traditions is known as galdr or galdur. Today, many believe the use of sung or intoned rune names in various combinations is galdur. Most likely, runes were a part of Norse and Saxon traditions of spoken and written magick, so the use of spoken runes draws upon an ancient tradition. The runes of the Elder Futhark are divided into three sections of eight. Modern practitioners have used the slow chanting of them, much like ceremonial magicians intone the Hebrew names of God, to create the sacred space of ritual. A very simple use of runic chanting is to move in a slow clockwise circle while chanting the names of the twenty four runes in order:

Fehu, Uruz, Thurisaz, Ansuz, Raido, Ken, Gebo, Wunjo

Hagalaz, Nauthiz, Isa, Jera, Eihwaz, Pertho, Algiz, Sowilo

Tiwaz, Berkano, Ehwaz, Mannaz, Laguz, Ingwaz, Dagaz, Othila

Specific runes or rune combinations can be chanted for more specific effects. For prosperity, one might chant the rune name Fehu, meaning wealth in the form of cattle, or the combination Fehu – Jera – Sowilo, for wealth, good harvest, and the Sun, all symbols of prosperity. For healing, one could chant Uruz for health, or the combination Uruz – Mannaz – Dagaz, for health, humanity, and growth of light. Groups of three runes resonnate with the three Norns of Norse myth: Urd, Verthandi, and Skuld, or past, present, and future.

Rune	Symbol	Magickal Uses
Fehu	ᚡ	Prosperity, Wealth, Power, Resources, Investment
Uruz	ᚢ	Health, Strength, Stamina, Opportunity
Thurisaz	ᚦ	Protection, Luck, Good Advice
Ansuz	ᚨ	Wisdom, Eloquence, Inspiration, Advice, Learning
Raido	ᚱ	Travel, Journey, Message, Control, Right Path
Ken	ᚲ	Energy, Power, Light, Fire, Lust, Enthusiasm
Gebo	ᚷ	Partners, Gifts, Love, Good Fortune, Union
Wunjo	ᚹ	Joy, Harmony, Blessings, Desires Fulfilled
Hagaliz	ᚺ	Hail, Limit, Upheaval, Unexpected Outcomes, Delay, Risk
Nauthiz	ᚾ	Patience, Necessity, Stress, Obstacles, Needs
Isa	ᛁ	Static, Ice, Loss, Slowing Down, Cooling, Separation
Jera	ᛃ	Harvest, Rewards, Peace, Fruition, Legalities
Eihwaz	ᛇ	Rebirth, Success, Questing, Perseverance

Rune	Symbol	Magickal Uses
Pertho	ᛈ	Fate, Mystery, Initiation, Magick, Future
Algiz	ᛉ	Protection, Friendship, Optimism, Aspirations
Sowilo	ᛋ	Sun, Victory, Honor, Achieving Goals
Tiwaz	ᛏ	Warrior, Sacrifice, Courage, Power, Energy
Berkano	ᛒ	Motherhood, New Things, Family, Creation
Ehwaz	ᛖ	Progress, Future, Travel, Movement, Change
Mannaz	ᛗ	Humanity, Altruism, Modesty, Creativity
Laguz	ᛚ	Emotions, Psychic, Water, Dreams, Intuitions, Reflection
Ingwaz	ᛜ	Potential, Fertility, Freedom, Conclusions, Consequences
Dagaz	ᛞ	Light, Growth, New, Breakthrough
Othila	ᛟ	Prosperity, Ancestors, Inheritance, Home

The use of the runes in terms of charms and engravings will be covered in a subsequent *Magickal Craft* book on charms, and the use of Runes as a divination tool goes beyond the scope of this series. An introduction to runic divination, and divination in general, from the perspective of a modern Witch, can be found in my textbook *The Outer Temple of Witchcraft*.

Barbarous words or barbarous names are magickal formulas, passed on in grimoires and rituals, that seemingly do not make any direct translation or linear sense. In the origin of the word barbarian, it simply meant one who does not speak Greek, though we now take it to mean someone who is savage. So barbarous words indicate words that are not easily understood and evoke a foreign mystique and power.

While in occult tradition we are admonished never to change the barbarous words, they are quite similar to the nonsensical speaking in tongues phenomenon. Perhaps they are a combination of spontaneously created words and foreign languages, used to generate power in ritual. You will find classic barbarous words in the next chapter from the grimoire traditions, but in theory, many random sounds and words can be considered magickal barbarous words.

In a similar style to the barbarous words is the banishment spell:

Hekas, Hekas Este Bebeloi!

It is usually translated to mean, "Be ye far, all ye profane." It is quite an effective incantation to banish unwanted and harmful spirits.

The use of such nonsensical words doesn't end with ancient times. We find them showing up in modern pop culture, and for the magicians who are either purposely inspired by pop culture as a modern myth, or those of us starting out who have no other resources in childhood and find things in the movies, television, and books, these can actually work as a focus for magick.

Two of my favorite modern magick words are used by practitioners to this day. The first is the "Charm of Making" from the Arthurian movie *Excalibur*. It was a powerful spell of Merlin's to raise the mist of the "dragon" or the power of the world all around us. With it, many things could be accomplished.

Anal nathrak, uthvas bethud, do che-ol di-enve

Though technically not truly Old Irish, it is said to be somewhat based upon an old Gaelic dialect, but has no cognate in historic lore. It certainly did not have anything to do with any historical or folkloric Merlin and Arthur. The translation is supposed to be:

Serpent's breath, charm of death and life, thy omen of making

While it might sound silly, I can't tell you how many people I've met over the years who have used it successfully as a focus, and have asked me about it, if it was real and if I had ever tried it. So many people asked that I had to try it on my own, and I found it an excellent source to raise energy in a spell. Despite rumors to the contrary, mostly credited to the highly critiqued and dubious book *The 21 Lessons of Merlyn* by Douglas Monroe, it is not an ancient Welsh spell, or ancient anything as far as any credible sources go.

The second pop culture example is the chant by Elphaba, the "Wicked" Witch in the musical *Wicked* in the song "No Good Deed Goes Unpunished":

Eleka nahmen nahmen
Ah tum ah tum eleka nahmen
Eleka nahmen nahmen
Ah tum ah tum eleka nahmen

So the tradition of barbarous words is alive and well in the modern era, and ready to inspire us in the next stage of spellcraft.

Exercise: Use A Traditional Incantation

Use one of the traditional incantations, either listed here, or do research to find another historic incantation you feel comfortable using. How effective was it?

Creating Your Own Incantation

While the incantations of others can be quite educational, and we'll survey more in the next chapter on historic spell lore, many modern practitioners wouldn't think of using only what has been used before, but will instead create their own, to speak to their own modern needs in magick.

If you are going to make your own incantations, here are some points to keep in mind:

Verse or Free Form – Will your spell be in metered poetry and rhyme, or more free form statements? Both can work, but many feel the pattern of poetry lends power to the modern day spell. If you agree, study the poetry of past magicians, particularly those wonderful verses from Doreen Valiente, well known for her rhyming couplets. To work, the incantation might not be great poetry, but it should convey its meaning clearly and succinctly. Don't use the excuse of great poetry for bad magick.

Evocation – Will your incantation call upon a particular divinity or other spirit? Such incantations can have some built-in power, but from a magickal theory perspective, you should establish a relationship with the entities you call upon. If you continue to call upon them without a relationship, they will either a) stop responding or b) seek you out and want something from you. A smart magician works those details out before a petition.

Memorization, Spontaneous or Written – Some prefer creating incantations prior to their need and memorizing them to use as needed. Others with a quick mind and quick tongue will

spontaneously generate an incantation as needed. A.
to use a small spell book of pre-written verbal charms a.
when needed. The spell book becomes a magickal device iı.
and a valuable tool for those with both bad memories and an
inability to speak in rhyme on the spot.

For those looking to improve their incantation rhyme skills, an
excellent exercise, used by some Witchcraft covens, is to accept the
challenge of speaking in rhyme for one whole day. For many of us,
we obviously won't pick a day when we go to work, depending on
our job, but we can find other days to accept this challenge. While
the result is a lot of bad poetry, it does help us think poetically and
increases our ability to rhyme on the spot and create magickal
incantations as needed.

Exercise: Create Your Own Incantation

While using the guidelines above, try creating your own
incantation. How effective was it? How similar was it to a
traditional form? Do you prefer your own to traditional
incantations? Are they equally successful for you?

CHAPTER NINE:
MAGICKAL SPELLS IN
HISTORY

History is full of magick. We find references to it in stories, legends and myths, and also in history books, by otherwise well respected philosophers and teachers. In modern culture, they either sweep these magickal theories under the rug as the beliefs of primitive people, or in the case of religious documents, describe such magick as miracles sanctioned by "God." But if we respect these philosophers' opinions on so many other topics, why not give a good look to their esoteric beliefs?

Along with philosophers and myths that reference magick, history has preserved a wide range of documents outlining all the practices of magick that have survived in some form to the modern day. Understanding our heritage of magick can help us integrate it more into our daily life as part of the human experience and not something totally alien and unusual. The lack of magick in the everyday life of most "ordinary" people is really an aberrant phenomenon in human history and one I hope will soon change.

Maqlu Texts

The Maqlu Series or Maklu Texts are a group of Assyrian writings detailing rituals of the ruler of Sumeria and/or Babylon to destroy evil sorcerers or sorceresses, sometimes translated as witches. The purpose of the magick is to both punish and prevent them from doing harm to the kingdom and priest-king. The term Maqlu is believed to mean "burning," referring to the destruction by fire of the effigies of these sorcerers. The text was first translated into German by Knut L.Tallqvist and then later, Gerhard Meier refined and continued his work. Ross Sinclair has since combined his focus on Babylonian magick with translating the work into English. The nine tablets represent a foundation of Western magick, with ideas and techniques still used by spell casters today.

My enchanter and my enchantress,
Sit in the shade of a porch made of clay tiles.
She sits and does her tricks, makes images of me.
I send against you thyme and sesame.
I disperse your sorcery, send your word back into your mouth!
May the tricks that you have created turn themselves against you!
May the images which you made resemble you!
May the water that you scooped be your own!
Your magic shall not come close to me, your word shall not reach me!
Upon the order of Ea, Šamaš, and Marduk, and the princess Belit-ili!

— Excerpt from Tablet V

Ephesia Grammata

The Ephesia Grammata are a series of magickal words and formulas very similar to the mantras of Hinduism and Buddhism, but in Greek. They would produce magickal effects when recited correctly and were considered ineffective if mispronounced. The Ephesia Grammata can also be inscribed and carried upon your person to be effective. They could grant strength or cast out demons. The words were said to be inscribed on a carving of Artemis of Ephesia, giving them the name.

Artemis of Ephesus

They have no immediate translation in ancient Greek, though many scholars have tried to translate them. One version of the Ephesian Letters in the Latin alphabet is:

Askion,
Kataskion,
Lix,
Tetrax,
Damnameneus,
Aision

These words appear in a variety of magickal texts in the Hellenic world to add power to various spells.

The Corpus Hermticum

The Corpus Hermticum refers not to a book of spells, but to a body of literature on spiritual and magickal philosophy attributed to Hermes, as the teacher Hermes Trismegistus, who is also usually equated with Thoth. The books primarily are a series of dialogues between teacher and student. The text deals with ancient alchemy and defends Pagan traditions as they were at least recorded in the Christian era, though some believe they can be traced to ancient Greece or Egypt. *The Corpus Hermticum*, sometimes referred to as *The Divine Pymander*, has provided a foundation for Hermetic magick, which in turn has influenced the modern magick traditions.

Here are the first five verses of the first of seventeen books in *The Corpus Hermticum:*

1. *It chanced once on a time my mind was meditating on the things that are, my thought was raised to a great height, the senses of my body being held back—just as men are who are weighed down with sleep after a fill of food, or from fatigue of body. Me thought a Being more than vast, in size beyond all bounds, called out my name and saith: What wouldst thou hear and see, and what hast thou in mind to learn and know?*

2. *And I do say: Who art thou?*

   He saith: I am Man-Shepherd, Mind of all- masterhood; I know what thou desirest and I'm with thee everywhere.

3. *[And] I reply: I long to learn the things that are, and comprehend their nature, and know God. This is, I said, what I desire to hear.*

He answered back to me: Hold in thy mind all thou wouldst know, and I will teach thee.

4. *E'en with these words His aspect changed, and straightway, in the twinkling of an eye, all things were opened to me, and I see a Vision limitless, all things turned into Light,—sweet, joyous [Light]. And I became transported as I gazed.*

But in a little while Darkness came settling down on part [of it], awesome and gloomy, coiling in sinuous folds, so that methought it like unto a snake.

And then the Darkness changed into some sort of a Moist Nature, tossed about beyond all power of words, belching out smoke as from a fire, and groaning forth a wailing sound that beggars all description.

[And] after that an outcry inarticulate came forth from it, as though it were a Voice of Fire.

5. *[Thereon] out of the Light ... a Holy Word (Logos) descended on that Nature. And upwards to the height from the Moist Nature leaped forth pure Fire; light was it, swift and active too.*

The Air, too, being light, followed after the Fire; from out the Earth-and-Water rising up to Fire so that it seemed to hang there from.

But Earth-and-Water stayed so mingled each with other, that Earth from Water no one could discern. Yet were they moved to hear by reason of the Spirit-Word (Logos) pervading them.

— *The Corpus Hermeticum, I.* Poemandres, The Shepherd of Men, Translation by G. R. S. Mead

Hermes Trismegistus

Greek Magical Papyri

This document is actually a series of fragments and smaller documents dating from 2 B.C.E. to 5 C.E. on papyrus from the Greco-Roman-Egyptian world. They detail a wide variety of spells, formulas, hymns, and rituals. The mix was typical of the syncretism of Alexandria, fusing names, images and techniques of Jewish and Christian mysticism with Babylonian, Egyptian, Greek,

Roman, and Mithraic magick and deities. The collection of texts ranges from more folk traditions and simple cunning ways of the traveling sorcerer to more complex philosophy and liturgy of a priestly cast or mystery tradition. Here is a spell for "assertiveness" given in the text:

xvi. Spell for Assertiveness

Greetings, Lord, You who are the Means to obtain Favor for the Universe and for the Inhabited World.

Heaven has become a Dancing Place for You, ARSENOPHRE',
O King of the Heavenly Gods, ABLANATHANALBA,
You who possess Righteousness, AKRAMMACHAMAREI,
Gracious God, SANKANTHARA,
Ruler of Nature, SATRAPERKME'PH,
Origin of the Heavenly World, ATHTHANNOU ATHTHANNOU
ASTRAPHAI IASTRAPHAI PAKEPTO'TH PA . . .
E'RINTASKLIOUTH E'PHIO' MARMARAO'TH!

Let my Outspokenness not leave me. But let every Tongue and Language listen to me, because I am PERTAO' [ME'CH CHACH] MNE'CH SAKME'PH IAO'OYEE' O'E'O' O'E'O' IEOYO'E'IE'IAE'A IE'O'YOEI, Give me graciously whatever You want.

— Papyri Graecae Magicae (PGM)XII.182-189

Curse Tablets

Curse tablets are a curious form of ancient magickal "literature" that survived due to the nature of the medium upon which they are transcribed. This does not refer to a specific book or collection, but a type of spell that has survived from the ancient world of Greece and Rome.

Essentially the spell is a binding or curse written upon a thin piece of lead, folded, often with a nail placed through it, and then placed in a specific location to make it potent, typically an underground location associated with the deity invoked. Hecate was a popular choice. These tablets could be buried in the ground, in graveyards or graves themselves, in wells, pools, crevices, or nailed to the walls of temples or sanctuaries. I know a modern proponent of reviving this form of magick. He lives in New York City and puts the tablets in sewers and gutters.

Much like a petition spell, they call upon a divinity for help, but most often to harm or inhibit another on behalf of the caster. Sometimes they were for love, or success, either to have the target fall in love with the caster or to have the rival fail. Many are for justice, calling upon a curse for a wrongdoer, thief, or vandal. They would involve magickal words, not from any translatable language, but from a spirit tongue that would be understood by the gods and spirit. This language and text was sometimes referred to as *voces mysticae* and is quite similar to other traditions of barbarous words of power.

Many well preserved curse tablets are found at the Temple to Sulis in Bath, England. Sulis was equated by the Romans with Athena. Many of these curses are for thieves stealing articles of clothing or other goods while the owner was bathing in the temple. More tablets were found at a nearby temple of Mercury.

Some examples of Curse Tablets are below:

Docilianus...to the most holy goddess Sulis.
I curse him who has stolen my hooded cloak,
whether man or woman,
whether slave or free,

that...the goddess Sulis inflict death upon...
and not allow him sleep or children now and in the future,
until he has brought my hooded cloak to the temple of her divinity.

Honoratus to the holy god Mercury.
I complain to your divinity
that I have lost two wheels and four cows
and many small belongings from my house.
I would ask the genius of your divinity
that you do not allow health to the person who has done me wrong,
nor allow him to lie or sit or drink or eat,
whether he is man or woman,
whether boy or girl,
whether slave or free,
unless he brings my property to me
and is reconciled with me.
With renewed prayers I ask your divinity
that my petition may immediately make me vindicated by your
majesty.

Sulis Minerva

Grimoire Tradition

The Grimoire tradition is a series of surviving European manuscripts, with pseudo-historical authors attributed to them, particularly Biblical figures such as Moses and Solomon. While the work is firmly rooted in the lore and worldview of the Jewish or Christian magician, elements of Middle Eastern and European sorcery and spellcraft survive in it. The patriarch authors attributed to the texts is meant to give weight and credence to the use of it in a Jewish or Christian context, even though the practices seem quite out of step with mainstream visions of those religions, then and now. Most famous of these are *The Greater Key of Solomon* and *The Lesser Key of Solomon,* which have become staples in ceremonial magick modern spellcraft and have influenced Wicca, Hoodoo and a variety of other traditions.

The term grimoire relates to the word grammar and really refers to a magickal notebook. The texts are not complete, but assume a certain foreknowledge of the practice. These would be the notes given from teacher to student, assuming that much of the instruction would also already be known, or verbally transmitted. Though generally reserved for European books, the style of book can be found across the world. Many European cunning folk, working within or outside of the tradition, would use copies of these manuscripts, adding their own spells, prayers and formulas from their practice.

Rather than focus on the spirit journey to commune with entities of power as a shaman might, they focus upon the summoning, commanding, and binding of spirits in the forms of angels, demons, and djinn. Seals and sigils would be employed to coerce and command the entities to perform in the end what might seem as more practical and worldly tasks, rather than lofty spiritual goals. The potential goals included power, riches, finding

The Casting of Spells

buried treasure, smiting enemies, and finding a comely woman. One of the few notable exceptions to this rule is the grimoire entitled *The Sacred Magic of Abramelin the Mage*. Many believed the grimoire itself would possess some kind of spirit or intelligence, able to transmit power or initiation by the use of the text.

Some grimoires were simple spell books, not used for spirit summoning. They included bits of occult lore, including secret scripts, philosophy, astrology, medicine, talisman creation, tool consecration, and ritual formulas.

The following is the oration and instructions on making a charm for favor and love, from **Chapter XV** of *Clavicula Salomonis*, or *The Key of Solomon the King*, as translated by S. Liddell MacGregor Mathers:

O ADONAI, most Holy, Most Righteous, and most Mighty God, Who hast made all things through Thy Mercy and Righteousness wherewith Thou art filled, grant unto us that we may be found worthy that this Experiment may be found consecrated and perfect, so that the Light may issue from Thy Most Holy Seal, O ADONAI, which may obtain for us favour and love. Amen.

This being said, thou shalt place it in clean silk, and bury it for a day and a night at the junction of four cross-roads; and whensoever thou wishest to obtain any grace or favour from any, take it, having first properly consecrated it according to the rule, and place it in thy right hand, and seek thou what thou wilt it shall not be denied thee. But if thou doest not the Experiment carefully and rightly, assuredly thou shalt not succeed in any manner.

For obtaining grace and love write down the following words

SATOR, AREPO, TENET, OPERA, ROTAS, IAH, IAH, IAH, ENAM, IAH,
IAH, IAH, KETHER, CHOKMAH, BINAH, GEDULAH, GEBURAH,
TIPHERETH, NETZACH, HOD, YESOD, MALKUTH, ABRAHAM,
ISAAC, JACOB, SHADRACH, MESHACH, ABEDNEGO, be ye all present
in my aid and for whatsoever I shall desire to obtain.

Which words being properly written as above, thou shalt also find
thy desire brought to pass.

In the grimoire known alternatively as both *The Black Pullet* or
Treasure of the Old Man of the Pyramids, various talismans are given,
along with magick words to be used. Like most grimoires, the text
seems to be concerned with using magick words not just to make
magick through spells, but to command spirits to fulfill your
wishes.

The words

ZORAMI, ZAITUX, ELASTOT

are used in a talisman that, "sets to work enough genii for the
immediate achievement of any work which the possessor may
desire to undertake, and for the stoppage of any which may oppose
him. The talisman should be of lilac satin with the figures
embroidered in shaded silk."

Celtic Incantations

In the nineteenth century anthology known as the *Carmina
Gadelica*, there is a wide variety of Scottish Gaelic prayers, hymns,
blessings and incantations, mixing Christian and Pagan magick.
The Carmina Gadelica clearly demonstrates how magick was part
of the daily life and worldview of these Celtic people, even in

Christian times, and points to the nature based roots of the ancient Celtic people.

Charm of the Sprain

Bride went out
In the morning early,
with a pair of horses;
One broke his leg.
With much ado,
That was apart,
She put bone to bone,
She put flesh to flesh,
She put sinew to sinew,
She put vein to vein;
As she healed that,
May I heal this.

Exorcism of the Eye

I trample upon the eye,
As tramples the duck upon the lake,
As tramples the swan upon the water,
As tramples the horse upon the plain,
As tramples the cow upon the 'iuc',
As tramples the host of the elements,
As tramples the host of the elements.

Power of the wind I have over it,
Power of wrath I have over it,
Power of fire I have over it,
Power of thunder I have over it,
Power of lightning I have over it,
Power of storms I have over it,

Power of the moon I have over it,
Power of sun I have over it,
Power of stars I have over it.
Power of firmament I have over it,
Power of the heavens
And of the words I have over it,
Power of the heavens
And of the world I have over it.

A portion of it upon the grey stones,
A portion of it upon the steep hills,
A portion of it upon the fast falls,
A portion of it upon the fair meads,
And a portion upon the great salt sea,
She herself is the best instrument to carry it,
The great salt sea,
The best instrument to carry it.

In the name of the Tree of Life,
In the name of the Sacred Three
In the name of all the Secret Ones,
And of all the Powers together.

The Yarrow
I will pluck the yarrow fair,
That more brave shall be my hand,
That more warm shall be my lips,
That more swift shall be my foot;
May I an island be at sea,
May I a rock be on land,
That I can afflict any man,
No man can afflict me.

The Casting of Spells

The Lacnunga

The word lacnunga means "remedies" and is the title of a collection of Anglo Saxon medicine, magick, charms and prayers in Old English. It shows how magick and medicine were entwined, and how medicines, particularly herbs, were empowered not only through their medicinal virtue, but through spoken charms, spells to be said as the remedy was being prepared and administered. The most famous of these is The Nine Herb Charm. It is not unlike the single herb charms found in the Carmina Gadelica, such as "The Yarrow," above.

Due to the Old English relying upon changing folk names rather than their now commonly accepted Latin names, the full nine herbs are somewhat of a mystery. A likely list of the herbs is:

Mugwort (Mucgwyrt)
Betony (Attorlaðe)
Lamb's Cress/Water Cress (Stune)
Plantain (Wegbrade)
Chamomile (Mægðe)
Nettle (Stiðe)
Crab Apple (Wergulu)
Thyme/Chervil (Fille)
Fennel (Finule)

Nine Herb Charm

Remember, Mugwort, what you made known,
What you arranged at the Great proclamation.
You were called Una, the oldest of herbs,
you have power against three and against thirty,
you have power against poison and against contagion,

you have power against the loathsome foe roving through the land.

And you, Waybread, mother of herbs,
Open to the east, mighty inside.
over you chariots creaked, over you queens rode,
over you brides cried out, over you bulls snorted.
You withstood all of them, you dashed against them.
May you likewise withstand poison and infection
and the loathsome foe roving through the land.

Stune is the name of this herb, it grew on a stone,
it stands up against poison, it dashes against pain,

Nettle it is called, it drives out the hostile one, it casts out poison.
This is the herb that fought against the snake,
it has power against poison, it has power against infection,
it has power against the loathsome foe roving through the land.

Put to flight now, Venom-loather, the greater poisons,
though you are the lesser, you the mightier, conquer the lesser poisons,
until he is cured of both.

Remember, chamomile, what you made known,
what you accomplished at Alorford,
that never a man should lose his life from infection
after Chamomile was prepared for his food.

This is the herb that is called Wergulu.
A seal sent it across the sea-right,
a vexation to poison, a help to others.
it stands against pain, it dashes against poison,

The Casting of Spells

it has power against three and against thirty,
against the hand of a fiend and against mighty devices,
against the spell of mean creatures.

There the Apple accomplished it against poison
that she the loathsome serpent would never dwell in the house.

Chervil (or thyme) and Fennel, two very mighty ones.
They were created by the wise Lord,
holy in heaven as He hung;

He set and sent them to the seven worlds,
to the wretched and the fortunate, as a help to all.
These nine have power against nine poisons.
A worm came crawling, it killed nothing.
For Woden took nine glory-twigs,
he smote the adder that it flew apart into nine parts.
Now there nine herbs have power against nine evil spirits,

Against nine poisons and against nine infections:
Against the red poison, against the foul poison.
Against the yellow poison, against the green poison,
Against the black poison, against the blue poison,
Against the brown poison, against the crimson poison.
Against worm-blister, against water-blister,
Against thorn-blister, against thistle-blister,
Against ice-blister, against poison-blister.
Against harmfulness of the air, against harmfulness of the ground,
Against harmfulness of the sea.
If any poison comes flying from the east,
or any from the north, or any from the south,

or any from the west among the people.
Christ stood over diseases of every kind.
I alone know a running stream,
and the nine adders beware of it.
May all the weeds spring up from their roots,
the seas slip apart, all salt water,
when I blow this poison from you.

Take mugwort, plantain, lamb's cress, venom-loather, chamomile, nettle, crab apple, chervil and fennel, and old soap. Pound the herbs to a powder and mix them with the soap and the juice of the apple. Then prepare a paste of water and of ashes. Take fennel, boil it with the paste and wash it with a beaten egg when you apply the salve, both before and after.

Sing this charm three times on each of the herbs before you prepare them, and likewise on the apple. And sing the same charm into the mouth of the man and into both his ears, and on the wound, before you apply the salve.

Another unusual spell in *The Lacnunga* is a Spider Charm. Due to various translations and interpretations, it has been seen as a charm against dwarves, the second in the text, as dwarves are seen as unwanted earth spirits, or a spell in the prevention against nightmares, spirits that "ride" us in dreams, giving us the popular conception of nightmares. Dwarves, elves, and other creatures of nature were assumed to be the cause of many illnesses. It's unclear if the dwarf takes the form of the spider, or the spell summons a spider-like creature to remove the dwarf, though an interesting interpretation by author Brian Bates involves the initiation of an apprentice wizard by an elder wizard, summoning a spider spirit, or a spirit taking on the form of a spider, to initiate the wizard.

Against a Dwarf II

Against a dwarf, one shall take seven little wafers, such as those one offers with, and write these names on each wafer: Maximanus, Malchus, Iohannes, Martinianus, Dionysius, Constantinus, Serafion. Then one shall sing the galdor written hereafter, first in the left ear, then in the right ear, then upon the top of the man's head, and then one who is a maiden shall go to him and hang it on his neck. Do so for three days and soon he will be well.

Then she ended it and oaths she swore that never this must injure the sick. Nor those with the power to acquire this galdor nor those who know how to.

Here come entering
a spider wight
He had his hame in hand,
he said you were his steed,
He lay his ropes on your neck;
they began to travel off the land,
as soon as they came off the land they began to cool,
then came entering the beast's sister,
then she ended it
and oaths she swore that never this must injure the sick
Nor those with the power to acquire this galdor,
nor those who knew how to sing this galdor.
Amen. Fiat.

Hindu Spells

Like any other mystical culture, the Hindu tradition is ripe with magick, charms, incantations, and spells. While many westerners tend to think of the Vedic traditions of spirituality as very lofty when compared to the folk traditions of European and African magick, you'll find that no matter where you go, in any time or place, people have the same concerns, and use magick to aid them in their life. Hindu magick spans the gamut of spiritual disciplines and simple folk spells, just like any other culture.

Some of the more lofty "incantations" might be around mantras, invoking the deity and planetary energies based upon sound. Others are more like the charms of other traditions. A whole range of love and sex charms, known as Strikarmani, are used to evoke love, manifest a spouse, gain sex, increase virility, cure frigidity, and keep fidelity. The following are excerpts from *Oriental Magic* by Idries Shah.

Rite to Arouse Passionate Love in a Woman
The user is instructed to make or obtain an "arrow of love" to hold when reciting this spell.

With the all-powerful arrow of Love do I pierce thy heart, O woman!
Love, love that causes unease, that will overcome thee, love for me!
That arrow, flying true and straight, will cause in thee burning desire. It has the point of my love, its shaft is my determination to possess thee!
Yea, thy heart is pierced. The arrow has struck home.
I have overcome by these arts thy reluctance, thou art changed! Come to me, submissive, without pride, as I have no pride, but only longing! Thy mother will be powerless to prevent thy coming, neither shall thy father be able to prevent thee! Thou art completely in my power.
O Mitra, O Varuna, strip her of willpower! I, I alone, wield power over the heart and mind of my beloved!

Spell for Arousing the Passion of a Man
I am possessed by burning love for this man: and this loves comes to me from Apsaras, who is victorious ever.

Let the man yearn for me, desire me, let his desire burn for me! Let this
love come forth from the spirit, and enter him.
Let him desire me as nothing has been desired before! I love him, want
him; he must feel the same desire for me!
O Matrus, let him become filled with love; O Spirit of the Air, fill him
with love; O Agni, let him burn with love for me!

By looking at this range of historic spells, it's easy to see, despite the somewhat alien trappings to our modern sensibility, the same basic human needs, wants, and passions. Spells for protection from curses, magickal power, the mysteries of creation, assertiveness, justice, favor, and love, are all sought by practitioners today. It's part of the human experience on some level, and magick has been a part of that human experience. Like us, those who came before spoke or wrote "petitions" calling upon divinities and powers and often used exotic words or phrasing. You might not choose to do magick in these formats, but knowing they are part of our lineage as magickal practitioners is important. And you never know when the magickal path will urge you to explore your history and seek deeper roots.

CHAPTER TEN: CREATING A MAGICKAL LIFE

While I believe magick is a life skill all should learn, because it is empowering to have tools to change your circumstances when facing difficulty, it's not the only reason to perform magick. Empowerment is a key. Many who come to me in my healing and consultation practice also see therapists and psychologists, but the repeated message I hear is that they like to have the ability to do something – a ritual, a spell, a meditation – rather than simply talking about their problem. Just to be able to take action is itself empowering. Some of my more skeptical clients say, with my encouragement, that even if it doesn't work, or even if magick is not real, it gives a focus on a potential positive outcome, and sometimes that's all you need. I find it funny to hear that from those who might not believe in magick, as that is the first step to magick – focusing on the outcome you want. Does it always work? No, but that empowerment, be it through a belief or an experience with rituals or simply a better focus until the circumstances do change, is the essence of what we do.

While empowerment and action are important, spells provide a foundation for developing a magickal life. Not everyone who does spell work builds that foundation, and while some actively argue against the union of theurgy, or religious/divine magick devoted to the gods and spiritual evolution, with thaumaturgy, the magick of folklore to make change, I see the two as inseparable. But as a Witch, I see everything connected and ultimately inseparable. That is the mechanism by which magick works.

Seeking to craft a magickal life has been important to me. To see the magick in every situation is to see that interconnection and to act responsibly to that interconnection and interdependence whenever possible. The magickal life is really the art, science, and spiritual path of living magick daily. You start your work in the world learning about magick and then hopefully doing magick through spells and rituals. Some of us learn it the other way around, delving headlong into doing magick, making a terrible mistake, and then going back to learn better. Even in those circumstances, the terrible mistake inspired us to truly learn our craft. Following the first two steps, we realize that everything we do is a ritual. Everything we do is a spell. Everything has intention to it. Our whole life becomes a ritual to fulfill the purpose of our life, whatever that may be.

Desire is Sacred

Unlike a lot of other spiritual traditions that teach renouncement, but hold more economic and political temporal power in the world than any organization dedicated to renouncement should, magickal spiritualities do not teach renouncement as the only path. We teach that desire is sacred.

If you have a desire for something, it is for one of two reasons. Either it will be something to help you fulfill your purpose, your True Will, or it will be something to show you the path of your True Will, by illustrating what is not your True Will.

If you do a spell for it, one of two things will happen. Either you'll get it or you won't. Like the continual branching patterns of roads, the crossroads of magick is where a decision must be made. In either case, you'll again have two possibilities.

If you receive your desire, you have to determine if it has been fulfilled and you no longer have that desire, because the desire healthily supports you on the path, integrated as a permanent change in your life. Sometimes the desire is fulfilled for us to see

The Casting of Spells

that no, it is not satisfying. What I thought I wanted was not really what I wanted, and I don't want to integrate this change into my life. I want to let it go completely.

If you do not receive your desire, you have to determine if it was faulty spellcraft or if there was another reason for failure. Was it because you held the spirit of the highest good, and this result is not for your highest good? If so, why do you want it so much that you'd cast a spell for it? Was the reason for failure that you have some self-imposed block to happiness or success? Why would you stop yourself from getting what you think and say you want?

Blocks to Success

We have all sorts of issues and complexes that can prevent us from fulfilling our True Will and receiving our Heart's Desire in the highest sense. These blocks prevent our different selves from communing. Issues of self-esteem and self-worth will rear their ugly heads. Many fear success because it brings as much change, if not more, than failure, and change is a scary thing. Some of us fear power or fear retribution through the Law of Return. We'd rather take no action than risk the wrong action. Issues of selfishness arise. We have a program that to be a "good" or "spiritual" person, we shouldn't really get what we want, that we are meant to suffer to be "good," and we all should want to be good. Right? If we focus our energy to get what we want, when we want it, rather than on the good of others, sacrificing our own needs, we won't be good. This type of thinking is inherent in many religious traditions we have been conditioned in, and is unnecessary and in fact detrimental to the magickal life.

Some take dogma from previous spiritual experiences and then overlay it onto their magickal spirituality. I see magickal spirituality, whether you think of the gods and spirits, or simply the universe, as a co-creative partnership. It's not based on religious piousness or moral superiority. I knew someone who was angry when non-Pagan people used magick in their lives, those who were not religious in their spellcraft, because she felt it was disrespectful and dishonoring. Though that might be true for her, if anyone is making helpful changes in their life, and the universe is responding to their intention, I think it should be encouraged. They need not be of my faith or even know the term True Will to find it.

It's all quite rich and fertile ground to explore for the conscious spell caster seeking not only to get results, but to be more aware on the path of evolution. Exploring and healing our motivations of why we do things, helps heal our past and get us clearer about our True Will and Heart's Desire in this life.

The Soul's Bliss

Mythologist Joseph Campbell is famous for saying, "Follow your bliss." I think that is the most important magickal advice anyone can give you. By following your blissful desires, you are being led to your True Will. The magickal religion of Aleister Crowley's Thelema put emphasis on Will, but also Love. "Love is the Law, Love Under Will," according to his holy books. In my own teachings, Love and Will are linked by Wisdom, appropriate knowledge put into action. These three forces are like the three selves of every human. We find our bliss when we work in conscious harmony on all three levels.

The three levels and the three parts of us living on them are called many things. Three is a very sacred number in most magickal traditions and religions, from Catholicism to Wicca. We can consider them the classic trinity of Body, Mind, and Spirit, with the corresponding physical, mental and spiritual levels of reality, though those words don't always do them justice.

In spell casting, we call them the Conscious Mind, the Psychic Mind, and the Divine Mind, paralleling the psychologists' conscious, subconscious, and superconscious minds. As we explore, we realize they are more than just "minds" and are really selves or souls, distinct, yet working for a common cause. We can simply call them the Middle Self, Lower Self, and Higher Self, as many do. Various occult traditions and teachings have specific names for them. My teachings call them the Namer, Shaper, and Watcher, respectively.

In esoteric Christianity, the teachings survived and were linked with the distinctions of the Body, Spirit, and Soul. Most people today don't make a distinction between spirit and soul, but technically the soul is the unique part of divinity within each of us, while the spirit is the part of divinity that is the same in everyone. Alchemists used the symbols of various chemicals, and for the Higher Self or Soul, sulfur was the symbol. It burns an individual flame. Mercury is the symbol of spirit, for all quicksilver flows into each, undifferentiated, like the Holy Spirit. Salt, the matrix, is the symbol of the body, the conscious human self. Alchemy and astrology would relate the Earth to salt, the Moon to mercury, and the Sun to sulfur.

In our daily life, the Higher Self has the Will, the True Will, to guide our life. It leads to the imagination of the psychic self, the intuitive self, to dream it. And our conscious self yields the result of the work. We just need to get the conscious self to more actively participate in the process, allowing the psychic lower self to unite with the Higher Self through magick, meditation, and ritual, just as the Moon mediates some of the light and energy of the Sun to the Earth.

Through a magickal life, you can unite the three selves and have them work in conscious common cause. When you do that, you've take a major step in fulfilling your soul's bliss, your True Will, in the world. From this point onward, the doors of magick are open to you, and many new ways of being are possible. The more people who open these doors and step through, the more magickal our world will be. Imagine a planet where all are actively fulfilling their True Will on a conscious level. The Age of Aquarius will rise fully and the Aeon of Horus and Ma'at as envisioned by Thelemites will take root in our world.

BIBLIOGRAPHY

Ashley-Farrand, Thomas. *Healing Mantras.* New York: Ballantine Wellspring, 1999.

Bonewitz, Isaac. *Real Magic.* York Beach, ME: Samuel Weiser, Inc., 1989.

Budge, Sir Ernest Alfred Wallis. *An Introduction to Ancient Egyptian Literature.* London: J.M. Dent & Sons Limited, 1914. Reprinted in US by Courier Dover Publications.

Cabot, Laurie with Tom Cowan. *Power of the Witch: The Earth, the Moon and the Magical Path to Enlightenment.* New York: Dell Publishing, 1989.

Carmichael, Alexander. *Celtic Prayers and Incantations.* Mineola, NY: Dover Publications, 2007.

Cooper, Phillip. *Basic Magic A Practical Guide.* York Beach, Maine: Samuel Weiser, Inc., 1996.

Crowley, Aleister. *Magick in Theory and Practice.* New York: Dover Publications, 1976.

Dyer, Dr. Wayne W. *Real Magic: Creating Miracles in Everyday Life.* Audio Cass. New York: Harper Audio/HarperCollins Publishers, Inc., 1992.

Farrar, Janet & Stewart. *Spells And How They Work.* Custer, Washington: Phoenix Publishing Inc,, 1990.

Flowers, Stephen Edred. *Hermetic Magick: The Postmodern Magical Papyrus of Abaris.* York Beach, ME: Wesier Books, 1995.

Hine, Phil. *Condensed Chaos.* Tempe, Arizona: New Falcon, 1995.

Mead, G.R.S. *Thrice Greatest Hermes: Studies in Hellenistic Theosophy and Gnosis, Volume 2.* London: Theosophical Publishing Society, 1906.

Morrison, Dorothy. *Everyday Magic: Spells and Rituals for Modern Living.* St. Paul, MN: Llewellyn Publications, 2002.

Penczak, Christopher. *The Inner Temple of Witchcraft: Magick, Meditation and Psychic Development.* St Paul, MN: Llewellyn Worldwide, 2002.

Peterson, Joseph H. (Editor). *The Sixth and Seventh Books of Moses: Or Moses' Magical Spirit-Art Known as the Wonderful Arts of the Old Wise Hebrews, Taken from the Mosaic Books of the Kabbalah and the Talmud, for the Good of Mankind.* Lakeworth FL: Ibis Press, 2008.

Pollington, Stephen. *Leechcraft: Early English Charms, Plantlore and Healing.* Norfolk, England: Anglo-Saxon Books, 2000.

Online Resources

http://people.bath.ac.uk/liskmj/living-spring/sourcearchive/ns4/ns4jcb1.html: April 15, 2014.

http://voices.yahoo.com/make-own-oak-gall-iron-gall-ink-home-school-2541484.html: April 15, 2014.

http://curses.csad.ox.ac.uk/4Dlink2/4DACTION/WebRequestCurseTablet?thisLeafNum=1&searchTerm=&searchType=browse&searchField=CurseNumber&thisListPosition=11&displayImage=1&displayLatin=1&displayEnglish=1&lastListPosition=%3C!--4DVAR%20records%20in%20selection[curse_metadata]--%3E%20:%20##%20Error%20#%2048: April 15, 2014.

http://en.wikipedia.org/wiki/Excalibur_(film)#The_Charm_of_Making: November 22, 2013.

http://www.evertype.com/misc/charm.html: November 22, 2013.

http://www.maryjones.us/jce/charmmaking.html: November 22, 2013.

http://www.musicalschwartz.com/wicked-lyrics-10.html: November 22, 2013.

http://realpagan.net/forum/topics/the-magical-use-of-psalms: November 23, 1013.

http://www.marktablerart.com/5.html: April 15th, 2014.

http://en.wikipedia.org/wiki/Abracadabra: April 15, 2014.

ABOUT THE AUTHOR

Christopher Penczak is an award winning author, teacher, and healing practitioner. An advocate for the timeless perennial wisdom of the ages, he is rooted in the traditions of modern Witchcraft and Earth-based religions, but draws from a wide range of spiritual traditions including shamanism, alchemy, herbalism, Theosophy, and Hermetic Qabalah to forge his own magickal traditions. He is the co-founder of the Temple of Witchcraft tradition, a non-profit religious organization to advance the spiritual traditions of Witchcraft, as well as the co-founder of Copper Cauldron Publishing, a company dedicated to producing books, recordings, and tools for magickal inspiration and evolution. He maintains a teaching and healing practice in New England, but travels and teaches widely. More information can be found at *www.christopherpenczak.com* and *www.templeofwitchcraft.org*.

The Temple of Witchcraft
MYSTERY SCHOOL AND SEMINARY

Witchcraft is a tradition of experience, and the best way to experience the path of the Witch is to actively train in its magickal and spiritual lessons. The Temple of Witchcraft provides a complete system of training and tradition, with four degrees found in the Mystery School for personal and magickal development and a fifth degree in the Seminary for the training of High Priestesses and High Priests interested in serving the gods, spirits, and community as ministers. Teachings are divided by degree into the Oracular, Fertility, Ecstatic, Gnostic, and Resurrection Mysteries. Training emphasizes the ability to look within, awaken your own gifts and abilities, and perform both lesser and greater magicks for your own evolution and the betterment of the world around you. The Temple of Witchcraft offers both in-person and online courses with direct teaching and mentorship. Classes use the *Temple of Witchcraft* series of books and CD Companions as primary texts, supplemented monthly with information from the Temple's Book of Shadows, MP3 recordings of lectures and meditations from our founders, social support through group discussion with classmates, and direct individual feedback from a mentor. For more information and current schedules, please visit: *www.templeofwitchcraft.org*.

CPSIA information can be obtained
at www.ICGtesting.com
Printed in the USA
LVHW051049261021
701572LV00011B/157